Academic Identity and the Place of Stories

Susan Carter

Academic Identity and the Place of Stories

The Personal in the Professional

palgrave
macmillan

Susan Carter
CLeaR
University of Auckland
Auckland, New Zealand

ISBN 978-3-030-43600-1 ISBN 978-3-030-43601-8 (eBook)
https://doi.org/10.1007/978-3-030-43601-8

This Palgrave Pivot imprint is published by the registered company Springer Nature Switzerland AG.
The registered company address is: Gewerbestrasse 11, 6330 Cham, Switzerland

Acknowledgements

To colleagues at the University of Auckland's Centre for Learning and Research in Higher Education (CLeaR, 2013–2020), thanks and aroha nui. You gave me the courage for this book, my intellectual, individual, quirky, open, and aesthetically and ethically strong workmates. Helen Sword, thanks for CLeaR directorship that made space for research writing and supported each of us to go further. Hinekura Smith and 'Ema Wolfgramm-Foliaki, thank you for your expertise and for your aroha as colleagues. Barbara Kensington-Miller and Sean Sturm, thank you for ongoing support, advice and manaakitanga. Thanks too to the sterling University of Auckland academics whose energy and commitment to excellence brought them into CLeaR's courses, and who brought with them the critical mass for ambitious teaching and learning; thanks to the ACADPRAC 702 2018 crew in particular—Andrew Withy, thanks for letting me reproduce your reflection on teaching, which makes a great example of the class's contribution to thinking here. The doctoral candidates whose journeys I shared have enriched my understanding of academia. This book acts as some kind of marker of the academic development we have done so well together.

Evija Trofimova, thank you for reading early drafts—your enthusiasm energised the book's production. Sue Osborne, thanks for your eye for detail and your warm common sense.

I acknowledge my parents, Frank Edward John and Edna Myrtle Carter, who need to be publically thanked for their unspoken commitment to values that underpin the book, and for making a small state house in Radnor Rd the centre-of-the-known-world, with its huge vegie garden down the back, fringes of flower beds—fresh vegies and flowers—linoleum polished by hand and always library books on the go. You performed a slow rhythm of steadfastness.

My sons, Rhys Blake and Damon Gareth, you gave me confidence when, as babies, you acted like I knew what I was doing. Then, as you got older, you were both capable, clever and self-driven children, so it seemed that I ought to be able to do things too. Thanks for being inspirational. My siblings Edie and Wally, Edie seeing the world as poetry, and Wal seeing adventure and jokes; the set of sister aunties laughing together and all talking at once over home baking; my cousin Hunt whose commitment to common sense and goodness makes her unusual in the best way: I could not have had a better family.

Neale, thank you for "getting" me… and then for hanging on to me. Sharing home and life with you somehow enables me to be less anxious and more open ended….

Contents

About the Author

Susan Carter At the point of publication, Associate Professor Susan Carter worked within the Centre for Learning and Research in Higher Education, Faculty of Education and Social Work, at the University of Auckland, New Zealand. She has given full-time support to doctoral students as a learning advisor from 2004 to 2012 (Carter & Laurs, 2014). She continues to be co-author and editor of the *DoctoralWriting SIG* academic blog (Carter, Aitchison & Guerin, 2020). Now, as an academic developer, she provides seminars and individual support for academics (Carter & Laurs, 2018). Her research investigates what is common across disciplines, with academic development work leading to interest in how to build, sustain and enjoy an academic identity and career trajectory.

References

Carter, S., Aitchison, C., & Guerin, C. (2020). *Doctoral Writing: Practices, Processes and Pleasures*. Springer Nature.

Carter, S. & Laurs, D. (Eds.) (2018). *Developing Research Writing: A Handbook for Supervisors and Advisors*. London/New York: Routledge.

Carter, S. & Laurs, D. (Eds.) (2014). *Developing Generic Support for Doctoral Students: Practice and Pedagogy*. London/New York: Routledge.

CHAPTER 1

A Fruitcake Imaginary?

Abstract This chapter sets out the book's goal, context, theories and methods while introducing the extended metaphor of the fruitcake imaginary. It locates the book's central topic of academic development in the context of pushing back against neoliberal pressure. It explains the unusual approach of this book: novel inclusion of stories as a performance of the argument being made. New materialism's interest in the body's contribution to understanding is expanded via theories of imagination to include individual mindscape. That leads to defence of exegesis as a research methodology. Indigenous knowledges demonstrate cultural reclaim from the business model of academia. Then each chapter is briefly summarised as an overview map of what the book covers.

Keywords Academic pressure • Stories within academic argument • Academic development • Imagination as tool • Exegesis • Indigenous knowledge

I started this book in the summer at a writing retreat, a CLeaR writing retreat enabled by a director who knows it is hard to maintain academic writing amongst the busyness of the semester, and who believes that academic writing is worthwhile (Sword 2007, 2009, 2012, 2017). It had been raining. With the wet Waiheke Island bush around us shutting out the world, we were talking about what we were working on. September 5,

S. Carter, *Academic Identity and the Place of Stories*,
https://doi.org/10.1007/978-3-030-43601-8_1

2017, I told my colleague, Ashwini Datt, that I was trying something radically different, with both stories and academic prose juxtaposed to pay homage to the imagination and to shunt together an argument about developing academic identity. The book would admix ideas that run through my previous work—about doctoral pedagogy, learning and transformation, academic writing and identity, and the tissues of emotion and interconnectivity that weave together academic existence. It was to be a culmination, and to be studded with stories as a way of performing its point. To defuse how risky and ambitious that introduction of stories into an academic argument felt, I joked that this would be "one fruitcake of a book." Our laughter together led to the decision that I should say, right up front, "this is a fruitcake of a book." Over the next few years, the idea of a mad mixture firmed up into the fruitcake imaginary.

The abstraction of the "fruitcake imaginary" stands in for imagined possibilities regarding academic development. The fruitcake imaginary is an extended metaphor that tries to span the intellectual richness of academia and kitchen-table homeliness of a family recipe, with a whiff of quirkiness from working across these zones. There's the literature and framework of academic thinking, rich with accumulations of research, and flavoured by theory. Game theory is here, and, with it, a penchant towards play as a deliberate method. Stories from life persistently wind through academicity to textually enact the interconnections between extramural life and academic career. Life experience is valued. A fruitcake is an inclusive cake. It is solid by merit of all that goes into it. The book closes by unpacking what the metaphor of the fruitcake imaginary offers.

That is the style; the content is about academic development. I'm an academic developer doing that work in this book as I do in my day job at the University of Auckland, sifting through academia as I see it, and looking for ways to enhance academic experience. Academic developers strive to "mark out and create safe spaces where we can engage in conversation about the idea of the university and find our place in it"—as they do so, they grow to "understand their own attachments to, and desires for, the idea of the university" (Fyffe, 2018, p. 364). Typically, the workshops I facilitate support academics who are seeking to improve their supervision, research writing, teaching and learning, and career development. I share resources and exemplars, and prompt collaborative learning with "students" who are actually colleagues, often with more experience than I have. My teaching focus, and now my research focus, is on how academics construct their identities, acquire their professional expertise and plan career trajectories. In this book I address questions that keep surfacing in my mind when academics talk about how their work is going:

1. How can academics step out of the sense of being always harried?
2. How can academic careers be steered to the realisation of their full potential?
3. How can academics have more fun while at the same time making the world a better place?
4. How can academics best weather the unsettlement of restructuring and change?

There's a need for this fruitcake of a book: academics are the new precariat, beleaguered, pressured, and often troubled when neoliberalism's focus on finance bulldozes through the ethics of pedagogy (Collini, 2013). Wheaton (2020, p. 67) reports that "global higher education is in a state of disequilibrium"; she notes a widening hierarchy in employment within academia, and a move away from Humboldtian values of public good to focus on the entrepreneurial university. Arguably, neoliberalism's propensity for change managers bent on change weakens academia's retention of what matters. "Dislocated, dismembered, and progressively unbundled, the public university today exists in a state of chronic fragility, servitude and uncertainty that has left it… drained of autonomy and agency" (Shore & Wright, 2017, p. 18). A litany itemising and lamenting "hidden injuries of neoliberal academia" cites the following as part and parcel of a successful academic career: "exhaustion, stress, overload, insomnia, anxiety, shame, aggression, hurt, guilt and feelings of out-of-placeness, fraudulence and fear of exposure within the contemporary academy" (Gill, 2009, p. 229). Seeking possible ways to sustain self-confidence and satisfaction within the academic working life, I draw on what I know, with a literature studies doctorate underpinning my years of work as a doctoral learning advisor and then as an academic developer. Besides sharing good practice strategy within this often troubled environment, I draw on an arts humanities approach. I propose that even within a constricted environment, or perhaps especially within a constricted environment, academics can more consciously use individual imagination as a compass—and that recognising this empowers the recuperation of autonomy, agency and pleasure.

The book takes academic development off the career path's route up academic promotion rungs, suggesting that instead careers can follow individual desire lines, "unofficial paths, those marks left on the ground to show every day comings and goings" (Ahmed, 2006, pp. 19–20), perhaps with deviance that proves to be positive (Marsh, Schroeder, Dearden, & Sternin, 2004). The purpose is to avoid becoming a "beleaguered, managed, frantic, stressed and demoralized professor" (Berg & Seeber, 2017, p. xvii). Allowance for possible deviation according to the dictates of the imagination may make an authentic, satisfying academic career more likely. The book's goal is to locate meaningful ways to build individual academic identity. Doing so requires self-fashioning and self-representation, the construction of career, life and self. Individual performance occurs within the framework of social affects, the frequent instability as "change managers" reshape the academic context.

Teaching a particular course, *Academic Citizenship and Professionalism* (aka ACADPRAC 702), within a postgraduate certificate of academic practice prompted me to think about how academic development can be fostered into deep-level satisfaction. Who do we think we are as professionals, and what are the responsibilities that citizenship calls forth? This book wriggled out from the thinking prompted by the course, and the practical exercises in text-boxes at the end of each chapter here are ones that worked well in that course, where we engaged in "collective biography," a therapeutic opening up (Taylor et al., 2020). These can be used in group work, in seminars for academics, or in private, for personal reflection. Talking to other academics, and sharing these exercises, I was advised to take care: the exercises ask participants to expose who they are and what they think. Many wouldn't feel safe doing that. (I can relate to that discomfort. I'm taking a gamble on empathetic readers in publishing this book.) Because I'd like suggestions to be useful in as many situations as is reasonable, I have added a second text-box to each chapter. Generally, one text-box on the page offers personal reflective prompts, the ones I used in *Academic Citizenship and Professionalism* with a group who knew each other well, liked and trusted each other, and enjoyed talking together from these prompts. The other box more consciously attempts prompts for interconnectivity, trying for safety.

My goal as facilitator has long been to go beyond instrumentalism towards finding a heart and soul in academic work, and this book takes that impulse further. The starting-point method in the course built from the ground up, prompting participants to hunt round in memories and cultural artefacts that mean something to them, firing up awareness of individual imaginations. That's the intention here too. Decades of inquisitiveness about academic identity come together here, from when I first came to university and thought all academics were marvellous, a rare subspecies, to now when I appreciate how hard earned that appearance of confident intellectualism is. My doctoral thesis investigated a motif within medieval literature: at my first academic conference, the International Congress of Medieval Studies, Kalamazoo, I loved the rich mix of medieval scholars–re-enactors who knitted steel wool into chain mail, tweedy Anglophiles, Goths in black and religious in a different sort of black–and the way they constructed quite variant individual readings of fragmentary tales, considered each other's constructs and built new understanding based on wildly variant contributions. There's power in difference, or, as Gerard Manley Hopkins exclaimed, "Glory be to God for dappled things… all things counter, original, spare, strange" (Davies, 1979, p. 68). Amongst what is different here, dappled and counter, this book also has stories in small slivers.

Stories are purposeful, modelling the fusion of (1) experience, (2) redaction in language, (3) inner mindscape and (4) outer performance. Stories add fiction's depth of field to the academic argument. If the fiscally driven university of the twenty-first century undervalues the study of culture and artefacts, this book takes an opposing position: it recognises that the driving force of culture energises academic work. My use of stories here insists on a link between the messy reality of lived experience and academic theory—the academic prose/story syncopation mimics work/life synergy. Donald E. Hall notes that, "Our lives are narratives entangled with other narratives, all demanding interpretation and response, and leading, through their intersection, interaction and critical engagement, to an ability to live differently and more ethically" (Hall, 2007, p. 21). The book offers suggestions for recognising and celebrating that the intersections with life provide each of us with resources for academic development. In the exercises provided here, you are encouraged to dig out your own stories, inspect them and perhaps tell them differently if doing so enables self-reclamation. If you do this in a group, you can run individual stories together, or bounce them off each other, bringing into being a bigger story of interdependence as survivors of the academic habitus. While much of the book focuses on individual reflection and self-growth, the larger intention investigates consolidation of strong academic networks that sustain.

Self-knowledge is the starting point towards self-purpose. Academics embody and perform their contribution to the university and thus society.

The capital we bring into our work is our composite selves. Higher education researchers accept that culture, class, age, gender preference etc. inflect learning and research, with rigorous theorising emerging from cultural (Guerin & Green, 2016; Paltridge & Harbon, 2006) and gender studies (P. Harris, Thiele, & Currie, 1998; Overfield, 1995; Rudd, Morrison, Sadrozinski, Nerad, & Cerny, 2008). Recognition of difference at this level is broad brush compared to the work that an individual can undertake in understanding herself, her specificity, the values she embodies and the sense of purpose that ripple out from those values. In Kearns and Gardiner (2007, p. 243), a sure sense of purpose was shown, surprisingly, to be the most important predictor of academics' perception of their own effectiveness and of a high work-related morale. It's problematic when busyness swamps that sense of purpose. This short book seeks purpose.

The next section steps through theory for justification of the book's approach towards locating and fostering purpose.

Theorising Academic Self-Fashioning

Theory about identity supports this book's aim to influence self-construction and from there, to suggest the importance of social networking within academia. From a fairly plebian perspective, research comes into being as the work of the logical mind. New materialism (for example, feminism, gender studies and indigenous studies) include the body, championing the value that sensate experience contributes when it allows the mind to critique social biases that map onto bodies. In a cutting-edge radical thrust, new materialists insist that we flip Descartean theory ("I think, therefore I am") to see that *being* ("I am" as the starting point) enables more nuanced, sophisticated and ethical thinking. New materialism shows how to understand, support and draw upon uniqueness, otherness and collectivism.

To the individualities of embodiment, and with a similar drive as foundational new materialism towards the worth of the personal, this book adds the individualities of the imagination. I follow Mark Johnson's (1987) use of the term "imagination" for the inner workings of the mind, its play and lateral connectivity. My argument rests on the assumption that imaginations are constructed by foundational myths and associated cultural beliefs, by art that makes sense of experiences, and by individual somatic encounters, by habitus and by the personal ideals that all these things teach, that sediment of myriad memories. As new materialists draw theory from the body (Ahmed & Stacey, 2001a, 2001b), I do from the affordances that the individual imagination offers to thinking. In practice, this endorses an exegetical approach, where the researcher applies their mind to unpacking a problem, allowing self-begotten research that does not rely on data but on individual readings of the world. Ethics committee approval won't be required. Exegetical readings shed light on "supercomplexity" (Barnett, 2000), the knotty intersectionality inhabited by different folk with different aims and agendas: when we share our individual exegesis it becomes possible to see both fine detail and wide spread. The first stage, though, is self-knowledge.

That should be easy. The body teaches the mind to see more perceptively; the accumulation of the body's experiences imprints the imagination; the imagination underwrites a vast sustaining resource. As Augustine put it around 400 AD: "All these [experiences] doth that great harbour of the memory receive in her numberless secret and inexpressible windings, to be forthcoming, and brought out at need" (Augustine, 1838, p. 189, 10.13). I'm suggesting that twenty-first-century academics can go into the labyrinth of memories that build imagination to bring out the items that might help in constructing a professional academic identity.

We can privilege the inner self, with its individual imagination, the thought driver that, in part, is founded on physical and emotional experience. Most importantly, growing conscious of your own uniqueness is enabling. It's an antidote to the imposter syndrome. Self-knowledge frees you to engage with others more openly and thus more fruitfully. Ironically, when we think about the details that build who we are and might be, individual self-recognition strengthens our ability for constructive relationships. Self-knowledge shows us how we are similar, how we are different, and perhaps knowing our own limitations lets us feel more empathy for others with theirs.

It helps to recognise, value and use your imagination in your academic identity development—then work interdependently with others towards shared satisfaction. Elizabeth Reid Boyd (2019, np.) notes that "Imagination charges the flame: it puts us in touch with our creativity, our life force. In a world of increasing global conflict, imagination has never been more important." For the purposes of this book, imagination is crucially important for countering, if not conflict, then academic tension, and that tension is global or perhaps glocal—both relating to individual institutions, the local, and to academia at large, the global. I build that argument through the book by looking at embodiment, family background, experiences, the values that these give, at stories, metaphors and poetic nuances to language meanings, at different theoretical constructs and at social networks and negotiations. The book draws on canonical English as well as academic literature, because literature, like most art, often touches upon hard but valuable truths. Canonical literature is my own inspiration. I'm an erstwhile scholar of English literature. I can only draw on what works for me, and you can replace my inspiration examples with ones of your own that are more immediate to you. The object is to find bulwarks against an encroaching business model of academia that might suck the soul out of our work.

It's not my intention to take on the topic of neoliberalism's agenda overtly (amongst others, see Wright and Shore, 2017 for that), yet that is the context that makes this book pertinent (see too Wheaton, 2020, for a more recent reckoning of neoliberal change). My argument here, and the intersecting fiction and practical recommendations, speak fairly simply to an antidotal humanising agenda. To push back on neoliberal constraints, and to emphasise individual imagination, stories are part of the book's mix: they perform my argument and contribute to it. The stories here emerged from different parts of my life—the last story, admittedly, from a dream. Each fictional item incorporates some of the book's academic suggestions.

Method: Exegesis, Language Play

This book offers an exegesis on academic development. The four research questions posed earlier are genuinely what motivated me to undertake this project, because academics invited to talk about their working lives so often expressed frustration, dissatisfaction and their sense of overload, and of inadequacy. It's a commonplace in higher education that a research project needs a problem or gap in knowledge to investigate, and often research questions are how we articulate that. Yet the questions that drive this book address phenomena that are tantalisingly busy, packed with myriad individual backstories. Higher education's "from research question to discussion answer" methodology doesn't seem possible here: there will always be multiple answers that work or don't work in different ways for different academics. What I *can* offer is not answers to questions, but a reading based on my own experience, and further questions that might prompt useful reflection that lets you find your own truths and answers.

This book follows the method I have defended elsewhere where I argued for exegesis to be accepted as a legitimate higher education approach:

> Simply, should you become aware of [higher education's] tensions, problems, possibilities, inequities, anomalies, or curiosities, [then] an exegetical methodology… allows the investigative and reflective individual mind to put literary studies methods into a field of play with each other. The results are thus subjective… an interpretive reading through an individual lens… (Carter, 2014, p. 126)

With an individual reading and some further questioning coming up, the book stretches genre to see what new cognitive potentials can be opened up when the imagination is given free range.

Although individual uniqueness will be a significant driver of self-construction here, my assumption is that, when we develop self-knowledge, self-recognition, and perhaps self-forgiveness, we are more strongly placed to contribute to networks, communities of practice, and to collegial relationships that are truly meaningful. I write from New Zealand, where indigenous methodologies and knowledges loan power to educational practice. "Whanaungatanga," or making a family-like relationship, humanises more theoretical constructs for functional interrelationship by making them homely. In one research team that was facing inward, to New Zealand, we drew on that concept in a research report (Carter et al., 2016, p. 37):

> Whanaungatanga is our starting point. Whanaungatanga can be interpreted, amongst other interpretations, as how we choose to practise relating as a family, and can be applied in all aspects where relationships occur, including where we study and where we work (see Chant, 2013). It is a Māori model that can help relationships between Māori and non-Māori. Māori philosophy of Pa Henare Tate (Tate, 1999) teaches that whanaungatanga is underpinned by the universal Māori values of
>
> - tika (doing what is right),
> - pono (doing what is right with integrity), and
> - aroha (doing everything with love/compassion).

In New Zealand where we often follow Māori protocol, I might introduce myself by acknowledging ancestors from Dalmatia, Scotland and England. That introductory habit of beginning with ancestors pleasingly assumes that doing what is right with compassion occurs upon a foundation of who you are, and which history of experience you carry in your genes and being, and must respect in your own performance. The same report was also dependent on the Pacific Island practice of "va," which we noted (Carter et al., 2016, p. 55):

> …the Pacific Island concept of *va* or *vaa* (Anae, 2010; Kaili, 2008; Thaman, 2008) provides a useful and meaningful framework for how we view the supervisory relationship between Pasifika students and their supervisors. *Va* exists in most Pacific Island cultures (Anae, 2010; Thaman, 2008) …to refer to the relational space existing between oneself and others and things (Kaili, 2005). Mahina (2010) categorises *va* into four dimensions, namely physical, social, intellectual and symbolic. All four dimensions are interrelated to one another (Kaili 2005).

The firmly collective identity of indigenous cultures makes a model that challenges neoliberalism's business model, and non-indigenous can make use of indigenous wisdom. We may not have that family and cultural framework ourselves as individuals, yet nonetheless might aspire to the richness of mutual responsibility in academic relationships that encompass the symbolic as well as the social and intellectual. In this book I aspire to find what is symbolic in what is homely. The use of stories to achieve homeliness insists that who we are as people rather than professionals matters, and that stories are strong evocative ways of teaching something.

Thomas and Reinertsen (2019, p. 195) explain of their book "Through the linguistic materiality and embodiment of writing, all the chapters are threads of entanglement, and these idea-threads will continue to entangle"—this book also employs that method of allowing "idea-threads" to tangle and entwine together. Weaving stories that reflect on life into academic thinking makes this something like "my true book, the one I should have written long ago" (Calvino, 1993, p. 166). Yet in writing such a frighteningly personal exposure of my own experience, I am trying really to probe *your* experience. If you can recognise and draw on your imagination, you may be able to have fun with others in the imagination's field of creativity and play. My suggestions for self-focused reflective practice are intended to be both provocative and restorative for academics who feel squeezed by the pressure of the business model of academia.

Chapter 2 begins with a story of failed learning to make the point that teaching and learning always depend on the life experiences of all involved. That establishes the personal as central to academic development. The Loathly Lady motif in raucous medieval Irish and English tales is used as a case study showing the method of using stories to influence. Imagination, metaphor, and the body's role in conceptualisation are discussed in defence of the book's approach to academic development as premised on the personal rather than on the institutional. Indigenous privileging of social aspects of research, *Kaupapa Māori*, and metaphoric world view build a case for the role of imagination. Game philosophy adds weight to academic self-fashioning, and the semiotics of language becomes a metaphor for building academic identity.

Chapter 3 looks at entry into academia, positing that perhaps the tension between academia's plush elitist lure and its relentless rigour could cause some psychological predispositions: desire, imposter syndrome and anxiety. The doctorate's transition leads into consideration of the different kinds of life experience that influence it. The roles of learning advisor and academic developer are described because these are the experiences that inform this book's methods—this book urges you to rake the roles of advisor and developer to yourself and your own development. A letter home tries to pass itself off as a story in Chap. 3—hang on, I want to change that to a more positive tone. It does pass itself off as a story, despite being a letter, and as a story that demonstrates the holistic nature of academic reality.

Chapter 4 homes in on the different arenas of academic work: teaching, research and service. It considers academic citizenship and professionalism. Acknowledging the messy reality that considerable academic work is invisible from audit scrutiny, it directly confronts some of the bothersome ironies of academia, such as when funding cuts run counter to institutional rhetoric suggesting socially responsible values. The chapter moves to consider how, amongst this mixed work environment, academics might find ways to advance the educational and social causes that matter to them. This chapter's story about a winter afternoon sports field shows different approaches to making the most of the habitus. The chapter concludes with emphasis on the personal, and on individual, maintenance of ethical values.

Chapter 5 directly confronts the instability of academic employment that is more common in the current neoliberal environment and considers how academics can best cope with changes that may be forced upon them. It draws upon borderland crossing theory, and on inspiration from medieval literature's constructions of heroism and leadership as those aspirations might be applied to academic endurance. This is a chapter about recognising what survives, able to be adapted. It suggests how professional identity and integrity might be held intact when subjected to institutional change managers at work. The story in this chapter pays tribute to longitudinality, to death, and to what we carry with us that we inherit from those who have gone before us.

Chapter 6 returns to the theme of a holistic mesh between life and academic career, insisting that personal values and preferences make good foundations for academic development. It includes a short exemplar from Andrew Withy, philosophy lecturer, on what motivates him as an academic. Imaginative intelligence is considered along with the potential of extended metaphors for reaching new understanding. The chapter includes some strategies for life that I have drawn from chess, sailing and literature studies to suggest that lessons from life make up some of academic identity. The story there is about a dance, again drawing on the potential of dance as metaphor—it's an old one: Geoffrey Chaucer was playing around with the "that art the olde daunce" somewhere between 1388 and 1400 when he wrote the General Prologue to the *Canterbury Tales* (see Benson, 1987, p. 31).

Finally, chap. 7 draws the book's themes together and provides the climax to the book. It returns to the issue of imagination's relationship with body, metaphor, and meaning-making, taking Mark Johnson's observation of imagination as the basis of reason further into imagination's creativity. Imagination and reflection are brought together. There's a tally of points that the book has made, with these points having been woven together throughout the book and now reaching culmination. They accumulate to a homily on a fruitcake, something homely and rich, designed to be shared, all of which is true of academic identity. The provision of the recipe performs emphasis on homeliness, heritage and community. The story is a dream with a weird futurity—make of its open ending what you will.

This book poses questions and provocations for reflection in text-boxes at the end of each chapter. Prompting reflection is an academic development ploy. Self-reflection, then, is likely to be helpful when used deliberately for academic identity development. Or academic identities development, since "the notion of a single 'academic identity' may be obsolete in an environment in which the academic role is becoming increasingly diverse" (Churchman, 2006, p. 3). Amongst the pressure of academia, and amongst this kaleidoscopic diversity of who we are and who we might be, we fashion ourselves.

References

Ahmed, S. (2006). *Queer phenomenology: Orientations, objects, others.* Durham, UK: Durham University Press.

Ahmed, S., & Stacey, J. (2001a). Introduction: Dermographics. In S. Ahmed & J. Stacey (Eds.), *Thinking through the skin* (pp. 1–17). New York, NY: Routledge.

Ahmed, S., & Stacey, J. (2001b). *Thinking through the skin.* London, UK: Routledge.

Anae, M. S. (2010). Teu le va: Toward a 'native' anthropology. *Pacific Studies, 33*(2), 222–240.

Augustine. (1838). The confessions of S. Augustine (E. B. Pusey, Trans.). In E. B. Pusey (Ed.), *The Confessions of S. Augustine* (Vol. 1). Oxford, UK: J. H. Parker.

Barnett, R. (2000). University knowledge in an age of supercomplexity. *Higher Education, 40*, 409–422.

Benson, L. D. (Ed.). (1987). *The riverside Chaucer.* Oxford, UK: Oxford University Press.

Berg, M., & Seeber, B. M. (2017). *The slow professor: Challenging the culture of speed in the academy.* Toronto, ONT: University of Toronto Press.

Boyd, E. R. (2019). How creativity can help us create moral imagination. *The Conversation.* Available at https://eveningreport.nz/2019/01/30/how-creativity-canhelp-us-cultivate-moral-imagination-101968/.

Calvino, I. (1993). *If on a winter's night a traveler.* London, UK: Minerva.

Carter, S. (2014). The methodology of magpies. *International Journal of Research & Method in Education, 37*(2), 125–136.

Carter, S., Laurs, D., Chant, L., Wolfgramm-Foliaki, E., Martin, J., Teaiwa, T. et al. (2016). *Research report supporting doctoral writing: He ara tika mā ngā kaiārahi.* Retrieved from https://akoaotearoa.ac.nz/doctoral-writing-feedback

Chant, L. (2013). *Hauora Kotahitanga. Maori health experiences as models for co-operative co-existence between indigenous and non-indigenous peoples.* Doctoral dissertation, Auckland: University of Auckland. Available at https://researchspace.auckland.ac.nz/

Churchman, D. (2006). Institutional commitments, individual compromises: Identity-related responses to compromise in an Australian university. *Journal of Higher Education Policy and Management, 28*(1), 3–5.

Collini, S. (2013). Sold out. *London Review of Books, 35*, 3–12. Retrieved from https://www.lrb.co.uk/v35/n20/stefan-collini/sold-out

Davies, W. (Ed.) (1979). *Gerard Manley Hopkins: The major poems.* London: J. M. Dent & Sons.

Fyffe, J. M. (2018). Getting comfortable with being uncomfortable: A narrative account of becoming an academic developer. *International Journal of Academic Development, 23*(4), 355–366.

Gill, R. (2009). Breaking the silence: The hidden injuries of neo-liberal academia. In R. Flood & R. Gill (Eds.), *Secrecy and silence in the research process: Feminist reflections* (pp. 228–244). London, UK: Routledge.

Guerin, C., & Green, I. (2016). Cultural diversity and the imagined community of the global academy. *Asia Pacific Journal of Education, 36*(1). https://doi.org/10.1080/02188791.2014.922048

Hall, D. E. (2007). *The academic community: A manual for change*. Columbus, OH: Ohio State Press.

Harris, P., Thiele, B., & Currie, J. (1998). Success, gender and academic voices: Consuming passion or selling the soul? *Gender and Education, 10*(2), 133–148.

Johnson, M. (1987). *The body in the mind: The bodily basis of meaning, imagination and reason*. Chicago, IL: University of Chicago Press.

Kaili, T. O. (2005). Tauhi va: Nurturing Tongan sociospatial ties in maui and beyond. *The Contemporary Pacific, 17*(1), 83–114.

Kaili, T. O. (2008). *Tauhi va: Creating beauty through the art of sociospatial relations*. PhD Dissertation. Seattle: University of Washington.

Kearns, H., & Gardiner, M. (2007). Is it time well spent? The relationship between time management behaviours, perceived effectiveness and work-related morale and distress in a university context. *Higher Education Research and Development, 26*(2), 235–247.

Mahina, O. (2010). Ta, va, and moana: Temporality, spatiality and indigeneity. *Pacific Studies, 33*(2, 3), 168–202.

Marsh, D. R., Schroeder, D. G., Dearden, K. A., & Sternin, M. (2004). The power of positive deviance. *British Medical Journal, 329*, 1177–1179.

Overfield, D. (1995). *The economics of social subordination: Gender relations and market failure in the highlands of Papua New Guinea*. Unpublished doctoral thesis, University of London, England.

Paltridge, B., & Harbon, L. (2006, November). *Intercultural competencies and the international experience*. Paper presented at the Communication Skills in University Education Auckland, New Zealand.

Rudd, E., Morrison, E., Sadrozinski, R., Nerad, M., & Cerny, J. (2008). Equality and illusion: Gender and tenure in art history careers. *Journal of Marriage and Family, 70*(1), 228–238.

Shore, C., & Wright, S. (2017). Privatizing the public university: Key trends, countertrends and alternatives. In S. Wright & C. Shore (Eds.), *Death of the public university? Uncertain futures for higher education in the knowledge economy* (pp. 1–27). New York/Oxford: Berghahn Books.

Sword, H. (2007). *The writer's diet*. Auckland, NZ: Pearson Education NZ.

Sword, H. (2009). Writing higher education differently: A manifesto on style. *Studies in Higher Education, 34*(3), 319–336.

Sword, H. (2012, July 23). Zombie nouns. *The New York Times*. Retrieved from https://opinionator.blogs.nytimes.com/2012/07/23/zombie-nouns/

Sword, H. (2017). *Air and light and time and space*. Cambridge, MA: Harvard University Press.

Tate, P. H. (1999). *Workshop on Whanaungatanga*. September 8–9, Auckland: Te Hiku o te Ika Trust.

Taylor, C., Gannon, S., Adams, G., Donaghue, H., Hannam-Swain, S., Harris-Evans, J., et al. (2020). Grim tales: Meetings, matterings and moments of silencing and frustration in everyday academic life. *International Journal of Educational Research, 99*, 101513. https://doi.org/10.1016/j.ijer.2019.101513

Thaman, K. H. (2008). Education in Pacific Island Countries. In G. McCulloch & D. Crook (Eds.), *The Routledge International encyclopedia of education* (pp. 413–416). London/New York: Routledge.

Thomas, L. M., & Reinertsen, A. B. (Eds.). (2019). *Academic writing and identity constructions: Performativity, space and territory in academic workplaces*. Cham, Switzerland: Palgrave Macmillan.

Wheaton, A. (2020). Shift happens: Moving from the ivory tower to the mushroom factory. *Higher Education Research & Development, 39*(1), 67–80.

Wright, S., & Shore, C. (2017). *Death of the public university? Uncertain futures for higher education in the knowledge economy*. New York/Oxford: Berghahn Books.

CHAPTER 2

Stories, Games, Language, Imagination

Abstract This chapter begins with a story of failed learning to make the point that teaching and learning always depend on the life experiences of all involved. That establishes the personal as central to academic development. The Loathly Lady motif in raucous medieval Irish and English tales is used as a case study showing the method of using stories to influence. Imagination, metaphor and the body's role in conceptualisation are discussed in defence of the book's approach to academic development as premised on the personal rather than on the institutional. Indigenous privileging of social aspects of research, *Kaupapa Māori* and metaphoric world view build a case for the role of imagination. Game philosophy adds weight to academic self-fashioning, and the semiotics of language becomes a metaphor for building academic identity.

Keywords Story as method • Exegesis • Metaphors • Game philosophy • Language semiotics

Chapter 1 explained the book's goal, context, theories and methods, and the "fruitcake imaginary" as an extended metaphor for the book's style and structure. Acknowledging academic pressures, it championed imagination as antidotal to the neoliberal business model, and forewarned that stories intersect here to invite the imagination to play. Stories are "crucial to the project and inextricably linked to its politics" (Berg & Seeber, 2017,

S. Carter, *Academic Identity and the Place of Stories*,
https://doi.org/10.1007/978-3-030-43601-8_2

p. xvi). They are used for their potential to allow more to be read into texts, including the texts of practice.

This chapter begins with a short story as an entry point to ideas about teaching and learning. This is a story about a failed-learning experience that taught me something about how to teach and something about the limitations and strengths of imagination. After that, I defend why stories belong here by drawing on literary studies analysis of their influences and affects in shaping identity. My chosen example to demonstrate this is the *Loathly Lady*, an early literary motif that unravels class and gender hierarchies. Power inequities within societies seem deeply entrenched. Yet this motif shows that western tradition has long explored issues of class and gender, and long recognised leverage for learning through playfulness. It's fun, and at the same time it does the serious work of bringing in the possibility of class and gender deconstruction with an early cultural consideration of them.

This chapter considers academia as a game. It encourages enjoyment of the play, and celebration of the imagination as a unique resource in creating a practice of play. The chapter finishes by redeeming the failure that the opening story describes, with an example of how imagination and metaphor can have practical traction. I also extrapolate, from considering syntactical mechanics for improving writing style, some principles for living a satisfying life as you develop your academic identity. That closure is exegesis at work: analysis of language mechanics (abstract ideas, nouns and verbs) in order to uncover the mechanics of self-construction.

* * *

Imagination; Numerical Im-Personation

As a child I could not learn multiplication tables. I could handle addition and I was even quite quick at long sums. Clumping up into bigger figures seemed a natural and honest thing for numbers to be required to do. You could see how that worked in the world: two shoes, four bananas, six children—that kind of thing. Addition was logical and homely.

But multiplication entailed a numerical engagement that looked problematic and possibly sinful. I liked going to Sunday school as a child, which might be why I suspected a sinister dimension to the verb ***multiply***.

Multiplication complicated the trustworthiness of numbers. My mum and dad were socialists who felt that those who multiplied money were all crooks of one kind or another, too.

And we played cards as a family, so I had the sense that numbers lived in their own world in a castle together with a king, a queen and a knave when they weren't in service in our world. The numbers in their own little castle world had characters. The castle-world construct was significant cognitive obstacle with learning how to multiply.

You learned about who the numbers were in their own castle world when they were multiplying. Five was the beautiful princess, selfish, because in relationship with others she demanded the status of a zero ending, yet another ring for those beautiful fingers, or else a reflection of her own image, the last word in five. For five it was all about five, take it or leave it.

Seven on the other hand was villainous, demanding outrageously improbable endings as a result of his relationship with others. He would have been the sadist, the addict, the bondage and car-boot man—had I known about those things. And, of course, a confidence trickster. He must have also been caddishly attractive to persuade a drab and rather dim handmaiden like four; the plodding servant, six; or the slightly elevated subaltern, eight, to take a whirl with him, when inevitably they would end up in a questionable situation like 54, or even, good grief, implicated by a line of associations in something as numerically sordid as 49. The even numbers were less selfish than the odd ones. Numbers onanistically multiplying themselves were a bit of an embarrassment, but you got an insight into who they really were when they did it.

Zero was a convenient number when learning about multiplication: it always left you with nothing. But everything it touched fell into a hole of non-existence. That raises some large, dark thoughts.

As a result of this approach to multiplication—my mother termed it an "over-active imagination"—I was one of a *special* group permitted to sit outside in the sun and learn times tables for the duration of arithmetic classes. We sat on the steps and didn't talk much to each other. It was peaceful, if boring.

The happy ending to this story, titled "Language: A Semiotics of Meaning-Making," follows towards the end of the chapter.

* * *

Learning, Stories, Teaching, Identity Work

In Defence of the Subtle Story

I'm calling the inserts through the book stories rather than declaring an autoethnographical approach because stories seem freer. In autoethnography, a personal story is then analysed as data, theorised, and thus legitimised by being turned into something clearly academic (Jones, Adams, & Ellis, 2016). The stories in this book work are not beholden to rules from theory as to what is permissible and what isn't. They work like stories, intending to interest and amuse you. At the same time, without much self-declaration, they weave in threads towards my overarching argument. What does that little story about the numbers' characters suggest to you? Something about how weird some learners are? Something about learner-centred pedagogy, and how you might teach times tables differently? Something about teaching in low socio-economic schools? (Are you an odd or an even number, and can you be both? Is sole authorship like multiplying with yourself…?)

I'm sticking up for the rights of fiction to intersect with academic research conventions. The intersection is a construct that allows fiction's conveyance of what it means to be human to interact with academic reasoning. The interaction occurs in your mind and imagination. I won't be spelling out the interconnectivity to you with every story in this book as I would if I were performing autoethnography. The story/research-writing mix allows under-the-table trade between fiction's reconstruction of what life means and academic extrapolations. This book about being an academic begins with the failed-learning story to acknowledge that learning occurs always within the context of each learner's life. That point is highly relevant to my overarching suggestion that you audit your own individual ways of thinking so that you can make best use of who you are as you interact with other learners.

Some assumptions run through this book:

1. Stories have long been vehicles that carry something to be learned.
2. What learners absorb over their entire life, from their accumulation of experiences, combine to mean that each academic is in possession of a lively imagination. Thus their academic work, teaching and learning, researching and writing, comes from a unique interpretation that can be overlooked.

3. Exegesis, the practice of interpreting what you read or see in search of deeper meaning, is a sound research method, because it enables academics to make use of their own unique inner minds, including their imagination.
4. If academia's audit seems to overlook the value of the personal, internal richness, we can celebrate it ourselves and do more to draw on it overtly.

Stories teach. The connotative workings of language in fiction can add layer upon layer of meanings, making more than one reading available and valid. Stories fuel imagination's work. They leaven the drabness of academic prose. They reorganise our thinking. An exegetical framework here emphasises the imagination's contribution to academic development.

Exegesis, that is, *interpretative reading*, is relatively common within arts, humanities, social science and education where the search is to add to understanding. Medieval literature scholars make the case that early stories were designed with subtle political agendas. What follows next is an example from medieval literature studies where academics analysed an early literary motif, the Loathly Lady, and concluded its main purpose was to influence the king, i.e., to teach him. Elizabeth Passmore shows how a medieval Irish court story ingeniously conveyed advice to the king, or king equivalent (Passmore, 2007). In a medieval hierarchy, it would be unwise to directly confront the warrior-ethos king with sound advice about politics: losing favour could be fatal. Good advice runs close to implied criticism. So instead, a funny, boisterous story with an implicit moral could sneak in advice. Passmore unpicks the Loathly Lady tale to show how that works. It's a pleasingly strange tale. There are different versions (see Albrecht, 1954; Benson, 1987; Macaulay, 1899; Ruggiers, 1979) including various ballads (Child, 1882; Graves, 1957), and from them the motif coheres: the Loathly Lady is grotesque—large, besnotted, pustular, with green tusks and talons—and she coerces a young aristocratic male into marriage, or sex, or at the very least, a kiss. When he concedes, she becomes beautiful, and in the early Irish versions (Stokes, 1903; Stokes & Windisch, 1887), she is *Sovranty* (*sic*) and Niall, the hero, wins governance of Ireland. His willingness to take on a nasty challenge shows his worth as a true hero.

This tale stands out because it so raucously sidesteps the generic norm. Knights, dragons, maidens beseechingly trapped in towers—medieval stories tend to have highly prescribed gender roles (Fellows, 1993). The Loathly Lady motif breaks the mould. Heroes in early tales frequently save a whole people by confronting a dragon, a monster, or an evil faery king, and they often win beautiful maidens as a reward. The confronting challenge from the Loathly Lady is much worse than usual: predatory female sexuality at its ugliest, viscerally described. Not only is the test unsavoury, it is ignominious and laughable instead of being admirable. And heroes usually overpower their challengers; that is how they win. With this motif, though, the monstrous hag who challenges aristocratic masculinity wins, and the hero saves his people and kingdom by doing what she wants. He wins by subordinating himself. That the challenger is a shapeshifter means this is clearly fiction, not an account of something that happened. Yet within the world of fiction, the space where imagination applies its force to things that happen or might happen, the motif opens up interrogation of prescribed gender roles (Carter, 2011). In her power and her initial unloveliness, the Loathly Lady motif might seem to be an early feminist push-back. Yet the story's female agency appears to provide humour that conveys a message to the king: a masculine agenda drives these stories.

The oblique advice to kings is to do whatever it takes to survive (c.f., Machiavelli's *The Prince*, 1513, edited Constantine, 2008); do what you have to do when your kingdom demands it; love and respect your kingdom for all its shortfalls; and learn to take (perhaps unwelcome) advice from unlikely sources. The hopes were that the king, drinking mead and laughing at the grotesque hag's cunning entrapment, would take in the moral and be more inclined to take advice from those beneath him, and beyond his inner circle. (And later on, this book in your hands develops the theme of taking advice from others, those outside of your own cultural framework, as a way of strengthening your academic growth.) In the Loathly Lady stories, Bakhtinian carnivalesque principles about the affective power of laughing could be seen at work (see Bakhtin, 1968, p. 921, who shows that laughter destabilises power relations). That so many stories have morals suggests that story-telling has never been neutral, but has always interested listeners in order to teach them. Stories, myths and legends, and cultural artefacts that spring from the imagination are foundational to deep-level teaching and learning (Carter, 2012). I'm arguing that we can do more with what we have learned from stories in developing our academic identities.

The submerged point that starting with a story makes is that learners have active minds, and imagination plays a role in learning. My story about an early failed-learning moment also hopes to trigger you to think about your own early learning experiences. What is it about who you are that means you learn some things readily? How did your imagination, your background, your experiences, what you read and what values you acquired from the complex mixture affect the topics you liked at school and those that perhaps still escape you?

As an adult, I can see the lure of mathematics as a semiotic system, and wonder whether we, numbers and I, could not have got off to a better start. I've learned from reflecting on over-active imagination and learning failures and successes, though. The context of this book is not the sunny primary school steps on which failed multipliers sat, but the *higher* education of academia. What I learned from considering things my imagination annexes, and things that escape it, helps me to categorise what is hard to learn in my academic work (so that I need to seek advice), and what is relatively easy, so that I am able to give advice and earn a bit of social credit.

Academia bears resemblance to a looking-glass world (Carroll, 1871) in some ways: intriguing and yet cut through with implicit rules that puzzle despite often conspicuously reflecting the tangible world. Ruth Barcan (2013, p. 1) notes that the sandstone gargoyles at Australia's elite universities, while grotesque, stake out a cultural legacy of intellectual privilege. She investigates the university as a place "riddled with contradictions–undeniably privileged, but fraught, fractured and pressured" (Barcan, 2013, p. 3). And for those working in this space, Barcan advises an approach to their situation that is "emotionally more mature, politically more astute, and ethically more sound than either bearing up or giving up" (p. 4). Now that I am an academic, an academic developer curious about how academics survive and thrive, how they develop leadership qualities that might allow universities to influence societies for the better, I am seeking possible routes to developing an emotionally mature academic identity.

Metaphors: Body to Imagination

An expert theoretician of metaphors, Mark Johnson (1987) began a book on the way bodily experience affects thinking by declaring, on opening:

> Without imagination, nothing in the world could be meaningful. Without imagination, we could never make sense of our experience. Without imagination, we could never reason toward knowledge of reality. (Johnson, 1987, p. ix)

Johnson (1987) goes on to show that spatial experiences of the body underpin metaphors to inform much of our deeper-level thinking. Imagination is thus enabled to play "a central role in the constitution of rationality" (Johnson, 1987, p. ix). If you are, like most readers, one who skims over large Latinate nouns, could you pause over that Johnson provocation? It's a chunky proposition to insist that the foundation and functionality of rational thought comes from imagination. David Punter locates further dimensionality that the metaphor carries: metaphor "also and crucially has a psychological dimension" (Punter, 2007, p. 73). He declares, "without metaphor, the world would have no 'sense'" (p. 81). Metaphoric sense-making takes us further than the affordances of rationality—into the realms of dream, art, creativity and religion, the realms in which we have the capacity for aspiration and culture. The human imagination, a foundation for thinking, can be given more acknowledgement for its power.

Metaphor and psycho-cultural significance hold ethical integrity of use in academia. In Aotearoa New Zealand, where I live and work, Māori and Pacific Island researchers have added the possibility of using their indigenous knowledges, approaches, and frameworks to research methodologies (L. T. Smith, 1999). Three aspects of this work draw me to champion it and to want to make use of these cultural contributions. First, the work draws upon things that really matter: "*Kaupapa Māori* has become a way of structuring assumptions, values, concepts, orientations and priorities in research" (L. T. Smith, 1999, p. 2). Secondly, there is a privileging of the social and communal aspect of research. G. H. Smith (1990, pp. 11–13) summarises the foundational pillars that comprise *Kaupapa Māori*. They include:

- taonga tuku iho (the *cultural aspirations* principle);
- ako Māori (the *culturally preferred pedagogy* principle);
- kia piki ake i nga raruraru o te kainga (the *socio-economic mediation* principle);
- whānau (the *extended family structure* principle);
- kaupapa (the *collective philosophy* principle).

Thirdly, indigenous researchers have a penchant for making use of metaphors, which makes their thinking accessible, vivid and compelling.

Traditional Māori greetings capture, in their poetics, very spatial positioning. A traditional whakatau, or introduction, is something of an extended metaphor about identity. A personal introduction begins by describing the place of family origin: "My mountain is…; my river is…; my ocean is…" and then works down genealogy. I'm grateful to Hinekura Smith for explaining to me that "many Māori metaphor move beyond an abstract analogous metaphor of understanding the target something through a source something and are more 'real' and embodied e.g the mountain IS a person and the river IS an ancestor" (H. Smith, private email, 28/01/2019). I think she's right—this is not my culture, but I feel moved by the power of its metaphors to reconceptualise. As Hinekura said, "it peoples the thing." The ritualistic invitation to a marae (meeting house) may invite "come, you with your dead, bring your bone-people to me with my dead." As non-Māori, I envy that this tradition establishes, right on first meeting, that the landscape patterns that shape imaginations have imprints that affect identity, and that individual ancestors also leave their mark: we carry the dead with us. Instead of beginning with a name, the label, the introduction begins with something closer to the bone, and to the heart. Envying the depth of these approaches, I am reminded to draw down on the roots of my own culture, and, if I am able, on evocative poetics that reach for meanings that matter.

Here is an example of how a metaphor can enliven the work of higher education. Wanting support for multiple teams with projects to improve Māori and Pacific Island success, two of my colleagues recently drew on a Tongan metaphor from ocean sailing: *pikipiki hama kae vaevae manava*. When a fleet of canoes heads to the ocean, if the sea is calm somewhere along the way, and if some of the boats are in trouble, sailors can *pikipiki hama kae vaevae manave*. That is, they can lash the canoes together and share resources, advice, stories, maybe swap the crews round so that each boat goes away again in the best shape possible. They may lash together for collective strength to ride out storms, too. 'Ema Wolfgramm-Foliaki, my Tongan colleague, sent an email explaining what the Tongan proverb meant and asking us all to put in time to *pikipiki hama kae vaevae manave* by helping lash the canoes (the teams of academics) together in a meeting to exchange resources, tips and advice. Their metaphor evoked the image of being on a canoe on the wide seas, the slopping of water over planks, wet skin, salt spray stiff in hair, banging the boats together and working quickly to lash them, pass things over… that request worked to raise enthusiasm and pleasure at being invited. The metaphor is not simplistic: "we / groups / cultures etc each have a self-sovereigning waka / vessel built on experiences, aspirations etc. The idea of *pikipiki hama* is not asking or insisting on us all getting in the same waka together nor does it assume that we are all '[paddling] the same' or are indeed heading in the same direction… unless we choose to … but to come together in ways that contribute to our growth before heading on our journeys" (Hinekura Smith, private email, 28/01/2019). There is that mixture of respect for individualism, self-sovereignty, embedded with a commitment to community, so "assumptions of shared community… [*and*] acceptance of differentiation and exchange" (Kogan, 2000, p. 207, my italics and slant on the quotation). Had the email requesting help said, "Could you please attend a two-hour meeting to give support to the research teams in a funded project?" we might have added the time to our diaries, but with less pleasure at the invitation. The poetics of the metaphor energised and motivated us. Language has force, mostly because it activates the imagination.

Other artistic media are also where the imagination strives to distil meaning, but this book sticks with language, because that is the medium I am familiar with, and because it is a medium of all academics. Almost unerringly, we are required to construct ourselves within research writing. Consideration of academic development needs to factor in the potentiality of language as a heritage alive for imaginations to draw upon. Although academia can be obsessive about rigour, it also makes a venue for creativity and provides scope for imaginations to work together towards new understanding. Academia makes a space for the magic of minds, for learning to occur, semiotic systems to flourish and new knowledge to be generated. These marvellous sleight-of-minds will be investigated in this book. Learners always have minds of their own; that is one of the most exciting things about human beings—and most complicating for teaching and learning.

To return to the opening story: the tale's small learner was programmed by Sunday school, by working-class socialist parents and by a stable, possibly cautious, family that played cards for leisure and release. The smallness of that beginning, a make-your-own-fun environment, developed imagination, a helpful capacity for lateral thinking. So yes, im-personating numbers as characters proved to be distracting from the rote-learning task in hand. Teaching and learning really do involve supercomplexity (Barnett, 2000), however, and if quirky personal approaches can be obstacles, they can also provide a spark. Packs of cards could be said to provide a metaphoric schemata still relevant to academia: as the song puts it, the gambler's "secret to survivin' is knowing 'what to throw away, and knowing what to keep'" (Schiltz, 1976). Well, yes. As academics, can we see ourselves as players?

Games

We played cards on an oak extension table in a rented state house. The most basic rule for all the card games we played was that if you couldn't lose graciously, you couldn't play—that rule defined family values and installed them in our family's young players. Game theory works well in academic identity construction too. Suits' (1978) philosophical interest in games is premised on Aesop's tale of the grasshopper who played all summer while the ant horded food for winter, launching a dialogue on the morality of play (Suits, 1978). Was the dull worker ant wise in following a survivalist pathway, or foolish in choosing survival at the cost of drudgery? Was it a tragic yet suitable consequence of frivolity when the cheerful grasshopper died in winter, or was it a triumph of the philosophical principle of choosing a higher plane of living despite dire consequences? Suits (1978) defines the difference between work and games, e.g., "games are goal-directed activities in which inefficient means are intentionally chosen" (p. 22); you cannot win if you break the rules (p. 24); and "rules are accepted for the sake of the activity they make possible" (p. 30). Suits (1978) points out that, in most games, contestants agree to do something a more difficult way than would be otherwise possible. Contestants run around a circuit rather than straight across it to the finish line. Golf balls are hit into holes with clubs rather than being put into holes by hand because *playing a game* is the purpose of golf, not effectively filling holes in the ground with golf balls. Given the rigour and rule-observation required to enter academic discourse communities, and the epistemological rules that demand a lengthy route to publication, it is tempting to reframe research writing as game-playing. To what extent is academic pedantry a game, and must we as a community treat it so earnestly? Could we turn that around to see whether academia as game offers a more optimistic frame, for example, for viewing academic writing as play rather than work?

Suits (1978, p. 148) cites Berne (1967) for the point that people play games for "social recognition." As I wrote this chapter, New Zealand went through a Performance Based Research Funding (PBRF) review, the equivalent of the United Kingdom's Research Assessment Exercise (RAE), and Australia's Excellence in Research for Australia (ERA). In these exercises, each academic joins a compulsory and serious game in which they must assemble a portfolio that demonstrates the *impact*, i.e., the social recognition, of their research. The process is time-expensive and can be tiresome and demoralising (Middleton, 2009), linked to neoliberal management of production. It is also a process where control of language plays a considerable role: publication descriptions that show impact are rhetorical exercises in talking up the significance of the work, but not beyond plausibility. Motivation to do this well comes extrinsically from the fact that funding for future survival rests upon your success and that it is a team effort to attract that money. The process is very much one of "joint enterprise, shared repertoire and mutual engagement which together explain how our work-related groupings support or undermine the socialisation and activities that define our academic identity" (V. King, 2003, p. 97). Many academics feel depressed when ranked for impact and output. One lamented recently that "they think we are battery hens." Yet failure to try hard at the exercise would let the team down.

While much has been written about the negative emotions that are released by academic writing and audit of it (some of it by me, and much that I cite often), it seems to me that acknowledgement of discomfort should move on to look for ways to relieve it. The social dynamic of PBRF energises self-audit. The time-expense is irritating, but, on the positive side, you articulate just who you are as a researcher, and have that researcher-self recognised: intrinsic motivation to speak yourself into existence can partner extrinsic motivation for survival, neutralising the sense of neoliberal squeeze. Rejecting the idea that intrinsic/extrinsic motivations are a dichotomy leads to the conclusion that "human motives are generically multifaceted and do not divide into just two types. … all human motivation arises from an intrinsic source" (Reiss, 2012, p. 153). We might pick up Suits' (1978) point that what is regarded as work is more easily resented, whereas what is regarded as play is entered into with enthusiasm and willingness to try harder. It helps, I think, to see the PBRF process and its equivalence as a game that you are paid to play rather than a bothersome demand that you are forced to fulfil.

Completing a PBRF portfolio, like most academic games, is hard because amongst possible impact registers, it's hard to know which the reviewers will privilege. Some on a faculty panel giving advice during preparation wanted researchers to spell out fine points of difference about their work; others recommended deleting prose in favour of statistics about citation rate and journal rankings. It is not new to see academia as a game made harder because some of the rules are not spelt out. Sharon Parry notes that "the idea that doctoral study is in a sense a game, or a meaningful social setting with rules, seemed bizarre at first… [but]… in fact, doctoral study does resemble the combination of written and unwritten rules in any complex game" (Parry, 2007, p. 237). In a situation where some game rules are explicitly stated in policies, strategic goals, graduate attributes and the like, and others are implicit at every level of play, there's scope for game rules to be tested and stretched. It seems to me that the concept of playing rather than working may be helpful in academic development. That includes playing with your imagination.

* * *

Language: A Semiotics of Meaning-Making

The sunny steps of failed times-tables learning that began this chapter lead somewhere—to the usefulness of the imagination's quirky connections. Although seeing numbers as characters prevented me from learning times tables, all is not lost; that is not the end of the story. The habit of hermeneutic reading, actively interpreting any text, was an inappropriate learning strategy with multiplication tables, and yet im-personating nouns and verbs helps in thinking about how to construct abstract terms in research writing, something I sometimes teach. Northrop Frye considers that religious understanding errs in designating God to be a noun, whereas, Frye proposes, God ought to be a verb (Frye, 1982). I like Frye's attention to the way that grammatical construction affects the deeper levels of conceptualisation. His suggestion rests on syntax's role in meaning-making as he spotlights the different implications of noun and verb forms. The difference is significant; they are arguably binary opposites (despite the equally arguable slippage that binaries usually have).

So when it comes to an abstract idea, the sort that researchers often construct as new knowledge or understanding, it helps to consider which syntactical form best conveys the meaning. Nouns are substantive. They are static. Their best quality is that they have presence. Their weakness is that they don't have legs; they cannot get anywhere without verbs. Verbs lack substance, but they motivate the world of nouns. They exert their own presence only by animating nouns. Nouns perk up and come to life once verbs engage with them. Once that abstract idea is put into the most accurate form, then the writing author needs to find a good partner for it.

When I am teaching this, I goof for a short time, impersonating the syntax. Nouns and verbs work together like functional couples. You have to feel that it is the verbs that activate the union. The nouns sit along one wall like girls at an old-fashioned school dance hoping that the right verbs will waltz them into purposefulness. The verbs always drive. Yet the nouns are entirely necessary. If a verb cannot secure a noun partner, it is just an empty gust or a shiver that no one takes seriously. The good thing about this is that, although both nouns and verbs have quite severe limitations, they work very happily together. Between them they provide the basic linguistic grid through which we conceptualise our experience of the world. Joking about nouns and verbs as characters at a school dance lightens the mood in a research writing class—I've written more elsewhere on the benefits of metaphors for defusing the tension when teaching writing (Carter & Pitcher, 2010). Once laughter relaxes the class, it is easier to talk about the fine tuning that syntax affords to clarity. When I teach what I call *advanced grammar* in a writing workshop for doctoral students, I ask students to scrutinise their habits with nouns and verbs as they pack their own abstract, complex or theoretical ideas into prose. We take the school dance metaphor further, to a macro-level, where verbs drive the nouns into contributing to an argument, the thesis. On the one hand, the substantive matter needs to be shrewdly chosen—but this requirement is secondary to the other hand's need for a live charge of argument throughout the thesis. You are likely to begin by feeling at the start of a doctorate that the substance matters most. In the early stages, when you envision yourself becoming an expert, you imagine yourself in possession of a *field*. However, acceptance that, actually, the verbal drive of argument is the essence of the thesis rather than its substance lets you animate the impulse that makes sense of them.

Away from multiplication's rote learning and towards language, voice and identity, extended metaphors work well for the "continual slippage between the person and the text" (Kamler & Thomson, 2006, p. 15). The way we construct ourselves in text, assembling nouns and verbs, creates a self upon the library shelf by which we are known. Some shelf-selves are blurry and uptight, whereas others become favourites. Higher education's discourse squelches with abstraction, which makes for rather stodgy writing. I don't claim originality with this criticism: Helen Sword has performed a quite brilliant anatomy of higher education research writing style, suggesting strategies to avoid the "impersonal, impenetrable prose that has become the dominant written discourse" (Sword, 2009). Sword's work is relatively recent (2007; 2009; 2012; 2017; 2018): there's a lineage of people who care about language (classics include Fowler, 1952; Orwell, 1946; Strunk & White, 2000; while Boice, 1990; Elbow, 1998;

and Pinker, 2015 are amongst many who bother about language and style). Education is also perhaps more appropriately a verb rather than a noun (and this is why it is so hard to measure teaching and learning with any degree of honest trading/academic rigour). Abstract nouns are much less vivid than concrete ones, and if you are able to slip in some concrete ones like "dance-floor" and "balcony" (Heifetz & Linsky, 2002), readers will welcome the sense of the real world coming back into existence. They are better able to join you at the balcony parapet and see what you see.

Some points about grammar usefully enable the revision of writing so that the ideas inhabit the most efficacious grammatical positions possible (Gopen, 2018; Gopen & Swan, 1990). The main clause should have the main substantive bit of the idea as the subject, and the main spasm of energy as the main verb. An example of a tautological main clause devoid of content is: "An indication of how far these ideas had developed and been generally accepted by the New Zealand public was shown by the Homosexual Law Reform bill of 1984." "An indication… was shown" exemplifies a verb idea, "indicate," being packaged up as a noun and then having to dance with a very close relative in the main clause. For passages that are clunky, or stodgy, or simply unclear, a door check of what is an authentic noun and what an accredited verb, and the banishment of imposters inhabiting inappropriate grammatical forms, can enable the meaning to be more readily apparent. In disciplines that draw upon what Sword (2012) calls *zombie* nominalisations (like transferability, generalisability), we do well to deliberately bowl these fat ladies round the dance floor with lively verbs (Sword, 2012). Despite the suggestive name, copular verbs (*is*, *are*, *was* and *were*, for example) are the drab dullards of prose. Sword points out that copular verbs are like equal marks in mathematics: they merely allow an appositive relationship to be established rather than shunting a movement forward (Sword, 2007).

I've elaborated on grammar in order to set up an extended metaphor that arrives at a moral for life—you should see Annie Lamott (1995) for an ideal book on writing and life that's a model for what I am attempting here. I suspect, at the end when we look back on our lives, it will be the verbs, what we did, that makes our life worthwhile rather than the substantive, what we owned. The purpose of developing your academic career, too, is that it allows you to develop as a person who does things.

The following text-box exercises nudges you to follow the model of learner-teacher self-analysis that I have demonstrated above. The first box is intended as introspection that you then use to give back into your own networks; the second, introspection for yourself.

Review your own childhood learning story: what troubled, bothered or eluded you, and what did you like about learning in your early years at school? Try writing a short story about you and learning that focuses on the irony of your own experience. What did you misinterpret at school? What did you really like, understand and enjoy doing?

Remember playing as a child: what games did you play, and what did you learn from them? Were the rules well established, or did you and your family or friends make them up or alter them? How did you agree about the rules (or did you)?

How do these childhood experiences underpin who you are now?

How does your own failure to learn make you a stronger teacher? And when was learning transformative for you as a young learner?

Revise your short story and preferably find an audience for it, a colleague or perhaps a class that you want to get closer to by breaking down the assumption that you know everything and they don't. Make someone else laugh.

What is the most innovative, imaginative, creative thing you have ever done in your life? What allowed or prompted you to do it? How did it feel?

What is the most imaginative thing you have done as an academic? How did that go? Could you share these two stories with other academics for the purpose of inspiring each other in use of the imagination?

References

Albrecht, W. P. (Ed.). (1954). *Thomas of Erceldoune: The Loathly Lady in Thomas of Erceldoune with a text of the poem printed in 1652.* Albuquerque, NM: University of New Mexico.

Bakhtin, M. M. T. C. (1968). *Rabelais and his world* (H. Iswolsky, Trans.). Cambridge, MA: MIT Press.

Barcan, R. (2013). *Academic life and the new university: Hope and other choices.* Surrey, UK: Ashgate Publishing.

Barnett, R. (2000). University knowledge in an age of supercomplexity. *Higher Education, 40*, 409–422.

Benson, L. D. (Ed.). (1987). *The riverside Chaucer.* Oxford, UK: Oxford University Press.

Berg, M., & Seeber, B. M. (2017). *The slow professor: Challenging the culture of speed in the academy.* Toronto, ONT: University of Toronto Press.
Berne, E. (1967). *Games people play.* New York: Grove Press.
Boice, R. (1990). *Professors as writers: A self-help guide to productivity.* Stillwater, OK: New Forums.
Carroll, L. (1871). *Through the looking-glass.* London, UK: Macmillan.
Carter, S. (2011). Mapping monstrous desire: Flirting with Sir Gawain. In N. Hoofnagle & W. R. Keller (Eds.), *Other nations: The hybridization of medieval insular mythology and identity* (pp. 165–184). Heidelberg, Germany: Universitätsverlag Winter.
Carter, S. (2012). Original knowledge, gender and the word's mythology: Voicing the doctorate. *Arts and Humanities in Higher Education, 11*(4), 406–417.
Carter, S. & Pitcher, R. (2010). Extended metaphors for pedagogy: Using sameness and difference. *Teaching in Higher Education, 15*(5), 579–589.
Child, F. J. (Ed.). (1882). *The English and Scottish popular ballads.* New York, NY: Pageant.
Constantine, P. (2008). (Trans. & Ed.) *The Prince: Niccolò Machiavelli 1469–1527.* New York: The Modern Library.
Elbow, P. P. (1998). *Writing with power: Techniques for mastering the writing process.* Oxford, UK: Oxford University Press.
Fellows, J. (Ed.). (1993). *Of love and chivalry: An anthology of middle English romances.* London, UK: Dent.
Fowler, H. W. (1952). *A dictionary of modern English usage.* Oxford, UK: Clarendon.
Frye, N. (1982). *The great code: the Bible and literature* (1st ed.). New York, NY: Harcourt Brace Jovanovich.
Gopen, G. D., & Swan, J. (1990). The science of scientific writing. *American Scientist, 78*(6), 550–558.
Gopen, G. G. (2018). How to improve your advisees' writing permanently—in 30 minutes. In Carter, S. and Laurs, D. (Eds.) *Developing research writing: A handbook for supervisors and advisors* (pp.77–86). London & New York: Routledge.
Graves, R. (Ed.). (1957). *English and Scottish ballads.* London, UK: Heinemann.
Heifetz, R. A., & Linsky, M. (2002). *Leadership on the line: Staying alive through the dangers of leading.* Boston, MA: Harvard Business School Press.
Johnson, M. (1987). *The body in the mind: The bodily basis of meaning, imagination and reason.* Chicago, IL: University of Chicago Press.
Jones, S. H., Adams, T. E., & Ellis, C. (2016). *Handbook of autoethnography.* London, UK: Routledge.
Kamler, B., & Thomson, P. (2006). *Helping doctoral students write: Pedagogies for supervision.* London, UK: Routledge.
King, V. (2003). Self-portrait with mortar board: A study of academic identity using the map, the novel and the grid. *Higher Education Research & Development, 32*(1), 96–108.

Kogan, M. (2000). Higher education communities and academic identity. *Higher Education Quarterly, 54*(3), 207–216.
Lamott, A. (1995). *Bird by bird: Some instructions for writing and life*. New York, NY: Anchor.
Macaulay, G. C. (Ed.). (1899). *Confessio amantis. The complete works of John Gower*. Oxford, UK: Clarendon.
Middleton, S. (2009). Becoming PBRF-able: Research assessment and education in New Zealand. In T. Besley (Ed.), *Assessing the quality of research in higher education: International perspective* (pp. 193–208). Rotterdam, The Netherlands: Sense Publishers.
Orwell, G. (1946). *Politics and the English language*. London, UK: Horizon.
Parry, S. (2007). *Disciplines and doctorates* (Vol. 16). Dordrecht, The Netherlands: Springer.
Passmore, S. E. (2007). Through the counsel of a lady: The Irish and English Loathly Lady tales and the "Mirrors for princes" genre. In S. E. Passmore & S. Carter (Eds.), *The "English Loathly Lady" tales: Boundaries, traditions, motifs* (pp. 3–41). Kalamazoo, MI: Medieval Institute Press.
Pinker, S. (2015). *The sense of style: The thinking person's guide to writing in the 21st century*. New York, NY: Penguin.
Punter, D. (2007). *Metaphors*. London, UK: Routledge.
Reiss, S. (2012). Intrinsic and extrinsic motivation. *Teaching of Philosophy, 39*(2), 152–156.
Ruggiers, P. G. (Ed.). (1979). *Chaucer, Geoffrey. The Canterbury tales: A facsimile and transcription of the Hengwrt manuscript with variants from the Ellesmere manuscript*. Norman, OK: University of Oklahoma.
Schiltz, D. (1976). The Gambler. [Recorded by Music City Roots].
Smith, G. H. (1990). *Tomorrow's schools and the development of Māori education*. Paper presented at the Second Educational Policy Conference, New Zealand Council for Educational Research. Reprinted in *Research Unit for Māori Education*, monograph no. 5, December 1991, The University of Auckland.
Smith, L. T. (1999). *Decolonizing methodologies: Research and indigenous peoples*. New York, NY: Zed Books.
Stokes, W. (1903). The death of Crimthann son of Fidach, and the adventures of the sons of Eochaid Muigmedon. *Revue Celtique, 24*, 172–207.
Stokes, W., & Windisch, E. (Eds.). (1887). *Coir Anmann. Fitness of names*. Leipzig, Germany: Hirzel.
Strunk, W. & White, E. B.(2000) *The elements of style*. Boston, Mass.: Allyn and Bacon.
Suits, B. (1978). *The grasshopper: Games, life and utopia*. Toronto, ONT: University of Toronto Press.
Sword, H. (2007). *The writer's diet*. Auckland, NZ: Pearson Education NZ.
Sword, H. (2009). Writing higher education differently: A manifesto on style. *Studies in Higher Education, 34*(3), 319–336.
Sword, H. (2012, July 23). Zombie nouns. *The New York Times*. Retrieved from https://opinionator.blogs.nytimes.com/2012/07/23/zombie-nouns/

CHAPTER 3

Academia as Unhomely Habitus?

Abstract This chapter posits the transition into academia as entailing tension between the attraction of intellectualism/historical elitism and the sometimes illogical pedantry. It considers what this means for teachers who care about first-in-the-family students and for first-in-the-family academics developing their careers. The role of culture, creativity and imagination are proposed as worth pursuing following consideration of early ideas about learning and spiritual development. The chapter puts forward the value of education in terms of deep-level individual development. The metacognitive work undertaken by learning advisors and academic developers is acknowledged as extremely valuable in the current secular educational environment. Textual self-construction in research writing is factored into academic development. Consideration of life's demands frames emphasis on holistic development, with a story demonstration of that mesh.

Keywords Transition into academia • Early career experience • Doctoral identity transition • Learning advisors • Academic developers

Entry into Academia: Learning Self-Confidence

This chapter contextualises the book's thesis, beginning with my reading of the entry process into academia. What portals are these, both attracting and excluding? The relics of historic elitism are compellingly attractive, I think. But the entry process is tough: the rigour of pedantry, the

S. Carter, *Academic Identity and the Place of Stories*,
https://doi.org/10.1007/978-3-030-43601-8_3

discipline, the doctorate's demand for new knowledge framed within a quite tightly prescribed genre. Many new doctoral graduands, possibly most, go through a phase living with imposter syndrome. Perhaps the foundational challenges of entry into academia are best named and acknowledged so that they can be defused.

Past elitism, in times when C. S. Lewis and Tolkien smoked pipes together over a pint in Oxford's Eagle and Child inn while haggling about theological implications for fiction-writers, leaves a legacy of plush entitlement. That legacy of intellectualism and privilege attracts many of us who partake of university culture. It is exhilarating to visit libraries like the Bodleian, the haunts of famous scholars, the grounds of old universities with their trees and gardens and to be there as a visiting scholar. Yet that rich, time-rosied tradition hands on an inheritance thick with inherent exclusivity, too. As one academic observed, "An old university… [is] nourished by a strong self-esteem" (Garret & Davies, 2010, p. 5)—the prestigious history and unquestioning self-esteem can seem intimidating too. Some academics have professor parents, but more of us come in finding academia initially baffling in its paradox of pedantry and intellectual freedom. We can find ourselves "cartographers mapping a geography of class difference… intensively concerned with language, literacy, and the power of the written word… [as we] reinvent [our]selves through language" (Zandy, 2005, p. vi–vii). A consequence of class discomfort is that "many experts want to wrap their subject and make it seem very difficult, and far beyond a normal person's understanding…" (Garret & Davies, 2010, p. 6)—that tendency gives a weak version of how universities might be. Many academics now are amongst the original massificators of education, the horde stampeding in for this luxury, and for the chance to measure themselves against something exclusive that was always so far beyond the dreams of parents. Sutton (2014, p. 5) attends to the power in rising above conditioning that is due to the effects of "class, gender and ethnicity… through education… and to move beyond it." Nonetheless, what attracts often also proves resistant. That is the essence of one problem behind academic development: how to generate self-confidence in what we plebs bring into academia so that we can find our most powerful selves to work from. Self-confidence is hard to construct when we are dazzled by the awe we can feel towards our disciplines and intellectual ancestors; yet we need self-possession and assurance if we are to stretch disciplinary boundaries with our different knowledges and strengths and if we are to make our best contributions with whatever it is that we bring into this plush environment.

I wonder whether the need for more confidence in ourselves should be expressed as a problem or as a potentiality that needs to be given the stage—emphasis on the value of individual imagination allows personal limitations and strengths to trade with each other. Academic development should lead to stronger metacognition (Flavell, 1979), that is, to thinking more directly about managing one's own development and gaining understanding as a reflective practitioner. The Chap. 2 story of failed learning counter-balanced by strong teaching has a place here because it makes the point that it helps to recognise the value of your own occasional failure, clumsiness and idiocy. Thinking about her frustration that, in her working-class home, academic work didn't count as work, and the grief that caused her as a young learner, Swartz acknowledges "Now, realizing what I had done to myself in college, how I had felt and why, I try to teach my students not to become fractured in the same ways I was because of language, racial, sexual, gender or class issues; for the same devastating social and political constructions that faced me then still exist…" (Swartz, 2005, p. 81). Academics can begin by recognising that the messiness and ignominy of their own pasts may help them to be more astute teachers, and are an important part of the resource from which they earn a living. The target for academic learners here, including myself, is to plot a career trajectory likely to give the maximum satisfaction possible and then to stay attentive to how well we do with that, and how we might do better. The exercise of critical reflection makes us better academics.

How can those for whom the university is an unhomely space (Manathunga, 2007) make full use of their individuality and their imaginative thinking minds in developing their academic careers? First-generation students, those who are the first in their families to attend, and who do not know what is expected of them, usually find academia discomforting on first entry. "For most of us from working-class families, it [the upward mobility of an academic career] is rather a zig-zag journey made possible largely through education, grit and luck, but not without loss and sorrow" (Zandy, 2005, p. ix). Academia's a place "often replete with remarkable intellects, passions, argument, politics… and prejudice—mostly based on an inheritance from the different disciplines that have influenced those populating the environment" (Garrett & Davies, 2010, p. 19). That can be a busy, shifting and shifty place, in which it is hard to orient with confidence. Unfamiliarity accounts for historic attrition rates and hence an institutional recognition that first-in-the-family students needed support to find their feet (Brailsford, 2011). Often life within academia remains somewhat alien even after moving on from the initial year to academic employment (and in recognition of the challenges, some guidance for academics is emerging, e.g., Cantwell & Scevak, 2010; Debowski, 2012). Even while pondering challenges, I stress that they are worth overcoming. On the one hand, one premise behind this book is that once you find out how it works, academia is where thinking-further happens outside of the box; a satisfying academic career is worth pursuing, and maybe we can make more of the open windows of opportunity if we are less daunted by their historic opulence. On the other, there are strict expectations for conformity, and for respecting the rules of the academic box. Before we can find windows of opportunity, we need to be inside the academic framework.

Teaching first-year students should entail showing them how this odd place works. Few people learn as children how to talk like academics. One third-generation professor once objected when, as a tutor on his course, I advised stage-one students to read their assignments aloud to themselves and try to get them to sound "like academics talk." The class knew just what I meant, but, to the professor, academics talked the same as everyone else. But he moved in well-educated social circles. Not all of us do (see Welsch, 2005). Academia talks its own kind of talk—it is a weird subculture, and we make it our own by adding its timbre to our own: "Being a 'working-class academic' is … like having multiple personalities and multiple minds about the same critical or mundane problem" (Atkinson, 2005, p. 92). Universities have moved on from the exclusivity achieved when only about 20% of people could make sense of what was being said at any given moment. Now that we have entered a drive for inclusivity, we have to widen the lexicon to include normal little words too. (But there are no *normal* words. Common words, then, and commonly known.) I continue to suggest that mimicking academic dialects is often how we begin to learn, and to rake in the A grades that build the foundation for an academic career. Eventually, you realise that you are genuinely doing what you once were tentatively copying…

Besides seeing how to produce the tone and timbre of academic discourse, there is a small heap of cultural expectations within the ivory tower that you do not know about until you are enmeshed within them. No one was this fussy about punctuation before you began producing assignments. The demand for literacy is fairly non-negotiable, in the way that restaurants that demand formal dress will not tolerate the lack of a tie. Those flamboyant, good-humoured academics who take a radical approach to their topics are unforgiving about the format of bibliographies; how could such wide-ranging thinkers be so small-minded about what is inconsequential? But format isn't inconsequential, you learn.

Another cultural prohibition that is particularly severe forbids drawing on previous ideas without accrediting them to their originator. In a bold challenge to the obsessive pedantry about who owns an idea, Lisa Samuels mounts a meticulously theorised argument that vigilance against theft of ideas has blinded academia to the principle of collaborative learning (Samuels, 2002). I've discussed this elsewhere (Carter, 2014), including, as here, a citation of the entire article, *Relinquish Intellectual Property*:

> If this essay appears to represent my own original idea, its appearance is undoubtedly false. Treating verbal ideation – the word – as "property" obstructs unsuspicious dialogue, clogs our minds as we try to delineate static "ideas" we call "ours," and falsifies the circumstances of knowledge. (Samuels, 2002, p. 357)

Craftily, Samuels, who is a poet as well as an academic, invites citation etiquette to be broken: I am able to cite her entire article without breaching copyright. That affordance is made available by merit of structure-as-conceptual-art. From an article that is only two sentences long, and its three-word title, Samuels hangs another 17 pages of footnotes and, her invention, "toenotes" that wriggle off the footnotes. She unpacks each word theoretically. In her very stylish article, Samuels argues that ownership is less the point than that ideas are shared as energisers for further thinking. As I wrote earlier, she emphasises what we all experience in academic lives:

> ...the iterative development of thought, the difficulty in delineating boundaries as understanding grows steadily over time. ...Samuels argues that the links between ideas, language, and authors are rhizomatic, and that obsession with fencing the entanglement diligently ought not swamp the ability to build new ideas. (Carter, 2014, p. 129)

Samuels' (2002) challenge aligns with my mission here of championing the thrill of imagination and shared intellectualism, perhaps over upward mobility, countable outputs and compliance.

Learners always have minds of their own; that is one of the most exciting things about human beings: that in the individual's processing of their own particular accumulation of experience and ideas, thought can develop, perhaps fired up by ideas from others. That energy of development is what matters most.

Nonetheless, like other academics, I take patient care when teaching to spell out cultural prohibitions and demands about citation with detail to students, because the relentless rules of academia are not always evident to those who rely upon their own experience, common sense and life skills. That my own background is working class, and that I did not know I was doing a degree when, as a postal worker, I took my first papers, mean I'm aware of how much needs explanation. I'm careful in this book with citation, including of my own previous words. Academia is shot through with irony: I can applaud Samuel's exquisite craft, and her crafty argument, and at the same time, I am not looking for trouble here. Or rather, citation questioning is not the trouble I am looking for.

Entry-Point Trial: The Doctorate

Because this book is about *academic* development, that is, the development of academics, it skips the captivating first-year-student entry point into academia and opts for the doctorate, the usual entry point into an academic career. And it is getting harder to get through that entry point: "the bar is being continually raised for each generation of faculty" (Berg & Seeber, 2017, p. xvii), with increased challenges that problematise the identity transition of the doctorate. Frequently, as part of doctoral learning, novice researchers leave their own values and complex individual thought-patterns at the entrance to the ivory tower in order to submit demonstrably to the epistemologies of their disciplines. I argue, alternatively, that the inner mindscape can provide an equal partnership with theories from disciplinary literature. And if doctoral students lack confidence to endorse the heart and soul of their imagination, we academics might become bolder from the vantage point of experience and the acceptance we have gained within our discourse communities. We can extend our approaches, responding to the idea that "the best way to illuminate the themes and issues of higher education is to bring various disciplinary voices into dialogue, even within one piece of research" (Golding, 2013, p. 155). The usual entry point to becoming an academic, doctoral study negotiates the cultural taboos, artefacts and customs of the academic subtribe (Becher & Trowler, 2001). Transition through the doctorate is an initiation, fraught with new challenges.

There are the puzzles of what research methods are acceptable to deliver enough data/findings for a doctorate. Research writing seems to need something called theory. Academic theory blesses the fortunate few with a new way of thinking that makes instant sense to them. bell hooks recounts: "I came to theory because I was hurting—the pain within me was so intense that I could not go on living. I came to theory desperate… I saw in theory then a location for healing" (hooks, 1991, p. 1). But theory is not always like that. Melinda Webber cautions, "any theory or ideology … can be liberating and it can be constricting" (Webber, 2009, p. 3). Webber notes the limitations of theory in holding true to experience. Life seldom fits neatly into theoretical patterns, and doctoral students often lack the confidence to challenge theorists, and expand or modify theory. In the worst-case scenario of being taught theory in dense clumps, it can seem a vast thicket that you are made to wriggle through, something that will never yield useful meaning.

Academic Writing: The Textual Construction of Self

Then, just the writing of a thesis is difficult. "For students, the problems of knowledge production, text production and self-formation are complexly intertwined at the point of articulation. Data analysis, principles of selection and focus, the structuring of text, the performance and defence of an argument are all questions of writing" (Aitchison & Lee, 2006, p. 268). The thesis needs structuring into a logical "story" that carries the equivalent to fiction's moral: an academic argument or position stake-out. There is a need for prose that demonstrates critical analysis, particularly challenging when English is not a first language. Thesis writing evokes extreme emotions (Aitchison, Catterall, Ross, & Burgin, 2012). What makes these requirements less like games and more like ordeals is the fact that the primary readers are the examiners, by definition reading to evaluate the success of the demonstration. I have previously conjured doctoral examiners up as lurking "amongst the dark things at the back of the cave, things feared to snatch away and devour the children of one's labours" (Carter, 2008)—a statement that is overwritten only because of how often I have heard unreasonable fear expressed about examiners as primary readers. Then many iterations of doctoral prose are usually called for to firm the thesis up against the examiners' interrogation, almost always much more drudgery than doctoral authors hope for. In short, writing a doctoral thesis is, as the memes gathered by Cecile Badenhorst and Cally Guerin show, a bit like walking into Mordor to tackle the dark forces of evil (Tolkien, 2001), and fraught with bad feelings, guilt and fear (Badenhorst & Guerin, 2016, pp. 3–10).

As each of us moves through the doctoral initiation, we learn a great deal about ourselves as well as about our topic. Academic writers learn to develop *voice*, influenced by discipline epistemology and discourse community preference, while the complexity of who they are is subordinated—or at least kept on a leash. Nonetheless, "the interests of race, class, gender, ethnicity, age, and any number of other related 'accents' intersect each utterance" (L. A. Finke, 1992, p. 13). Who we *are* matters. Research investigating some of these aspects will thread through this book, picking through the complexity and potential of academic identity, writerly voice and the wild magic of the mind.

Life (Academic Life) and Its Players: Gender, Class and Cultural Effects

Who you are governs the transition of the doctorate. Life presses and penetrates academic work. Women can find this especially hard (Carter, Blumenstein, & Cook, 2013): societies still often gender them as principal caregivers in the home. So they are expected to be wonderful cooks, affectionate wives, and child-focused mothers at home; at university, they must meet deadlines while being sharp-edged and critical (sleeplessness is a cost, argue Acker and Armenti, 2004). Yet, despite working hard to keep everyone happy, and hopping across roles, they can find that they are always seen as, and probably feel themselves to be, inadequate wives, bad mothers and disappointing doctoral students. Probably, rather than gender per se, it is being a parent that pushes women into disadvantage (Brown & Watson, 2010). Furthermore, as they step slowly into the role of world expert in a niche within their field, women's newly developed academic authority may undermine relationships that were established when they were soft, more subordinate and feminine (Carter et al., 2013). Being a topic authority requires academics to step forward and speak. In middle-class, well-educated western sub-cultures, this is a norm. It is not, though, in many communities, and it is too easy for academics, talking usually to their own kind, to forget that the world is not universal. Those of us who applaud feminism need to see how hard it is for some women to step into "the flirtatiousness of intellectual debate, in the game of competing, [and]... the sexiness of winning..." (Kirby, 1994, p. 19) when they come from cultures and sub-cultures that punish females who are visible and strident, let alone competing successfully with men.

Other aspects of embodiment influence comfort within academia. One study's title evokes powerful ambiguity to the link between body and mind: "thinking through the skin" (Sara Ahmed & Jackie Stacey, 2001a, 2001b, titular). As Ahmed and Stacey theorised what skin means, they make a case for the significance of the physical, i.e., race and gender preference, building an argument that embodiment provides perspective, and a research framework that counters social bias. The skin as a metonym for the body "has multiple histories and unimaginable futures" (Ahmed & Stacey, 2001a, 2001b, p. 2). Histories and futures are tied into social values, and societies construct people by evaluation of them. This is often premised upon bodies: as Ahmed and Stacey insist, "the skin is always open to being read"; it is "written and narrated… managed by subjects and others…" (Ahmed & Stacey, 2001a, 2001b, pp. 1–2). Ahmed and Stacey's (2001a, 2001b) work "reflects not on the body as the lost object to thought, but on inter-embodiment, on the mode of being-with and being-for, where one touches and is touched by others" (p. 1). Webber (2009) notes that Māori, New Zealand's indigenous people, are constructed both subjectively through political consciousness and voice, and objectively through biology and cultural background, and finds that "defining who Māori are has rarely been a neutral site, but one… vigorously debated and contested" (p. 2). An embodied perspective, moderated by all the experiences of gender, age and culture, can situate scholars within the controversies of their fields. And I'm factoring in the role of the imagination to the mixture of body and mind. Heart and soul deserve consideration, too, in thinking about teaching and learning (and what different learners, teachers and researchers bring to that work). Bodies, biases and being variously matter within academia, sometimes problematically, and often with the potential for empowerment. Struggles occur in transition into the university, into postgraduate study, into researcher independences and into academic identities. This book follows Ahmed and Stacy's (2001a, 2001b) assumption that knowing and endorsing yourself improve your capacity for relationships with others.

Indigenous writers too can find academe's underpinning western assumptions unwelcoming, and they historically take longer to complete degrees: Theodore et al. (2016) showed Māori "under-represented as graduates, particularly as postgraduates", while finding that although the majority of Māori graduates studied full-time, they also often worked while studying, with one third also raising a family (32.9%), while nearly half were first-generation students (48.4%) (p. 604). Of these, "females were more likely to be parents, to study extramurally, to work part time, and to have a long-term medical condition, impairment or disability" (p. 609). Yet the world views, knowledges and pedagogies these people bring into western discourse enrich it. Sometimes the voice from the

South Pacific is refreshingly honest and willing to laugh at self as well as at academia. A recognised leader in higher education critiqued research funding systems and ascribed pejoratives to himself as a funded researcher that are clearly untrue or at least wildly exaggerated: "Neotraditionalism ... touted by westernised, urbanised elite groups is abysmally narrow-minded and has recently proved itself to be unconscionably racist. I'm hypocritical, corrupt, self-centred and fraudulent. So it takes a thief to catch a thief..." (Hau'ofa, 2008, p. 150). My ears prick up when I hear skill with witty critique—that seems so like the humour I associate with workers, so refreshing compared with the stilted guardedness of most academic rhetoric. When indigenous academics feel comfortable enough to draw on culturally honed skill-sets, they make academia a world we might all want to live in.

Along with a wry, irreverent humour, Māori and Pacific Island frameworks bring personal interconnections into play, for example, providing a good model of supervision. They mostly do this by means of metaphors about family and relational space. Those within the cultures will recognise the familiar, and additionally, those of us who are outsiders will notice the power of those metaphors to push back against the neoliberal accountability agenda (Carter, Laurs, Chant, & Wolgramm-Foliaki, 2017). Potent with push-back, "creativity... arises from cultural borrowing and transactions" (Negus & Pickering, 2004, p. 40). The terms whanaungatanga (making a family-like relationship) and va (maintaining the relational space between people and between people and objects) implicitly bring supervision back to being about people working together on projects in the particularities of time and space rather than being about outputs. Making use of grounded metaphors brings the concrete into academia, making it more inviting and more habitable. A fast finish launches ideas and careers, and for that reason, it is ideal, but speed is not the primary issue relating to the doctorate and its supervision. In arts, humanities and social sciences it is crucial that a wide range of perspectives speak within discourses—we need multiple readings to gain any sense of a full picture. Compassion for those historically under-represented in success is not the main motivator here, but the need for research to tap as full an understanding as possible. We need their knowledges. "It is then through a heightened sense of creativity and the apparent trivialities of everyday living that we may come to see what is extraordinary in ordinary life, and what is strange in mundane familiarity" (Negus & Pickering, 2004, p. 45).

Learning Advisors and Academic Developers: A Metacognitive Overview of the Field of Play

Engagement with the *variety* of learners who are caught up in tertiary education is the central work of learning advisors, the term given to those who work with students, and academic developers, and the term given to those who work with academics. I've done both these jobs, making what I have learned by doing so an area of education expertise. Learning advisors do not teach subjects, but rather they teach the metacognitive skills of learning (Carter & Laurs, 2014). They unlock the puzzles of academia, explaining what is expected by this strangely brachiated culture. Teachers within disciplines may be aware of disciplinary threshold concepts. Learning advisors encourage students' conceptual threshold crossing, showing how to learn and take charge of self-development. Although scholars research education's teaching and learning from many different approaches, behind the laboratory of the classroom, networks of thought and life experience feed in and out of learning. Imaginations, those thinking minds that make sense of the world and make the world, develop thus. I'm factoring in awareness of the potent interconnectivity between research thinking and thinking as a neighbour, a tenant, a mother, a partner… Consultation with a learning advisor often lets a student explain the life/study mixture, not only to whinge about it, but also, sometimes, to notice the potential that life offers for scholarly sustenance.

Then, academic developers fulfil a similar role to learning advisors, only with academics rather than students, showing how to teach, publish, supervise and, at the metacognitive level, survive. The two roles are similar at the level of personal growth. Academic developers respond to the fact that academics are still learners. Although academics may have "thought they had crossed the threshold to become teachers, authorities, they are thrown back into the uncertain condition of being novices and learners" (Grant & Barrow, 2013, p. 312) quite commonly, as the academic environment demands new kinds of work, different personalities to work with, and new decisions as to how much of themselves they want to bring into their career. While figuring out how to prompt the learning needed to thrive, academic developers create a safe marginal space where academics can talk honestly with each other and share strategies "away from unruly students, difficult ideas, the formal pedagogies of the lecture and the laboratory…" (Grant & Barrow, 2013, p. 313). Grant and Barrow read academic teacher development seminars as Lacanian heterotopias (p. 308). They flatly state that because staff seminars cross disciplines, they are effectively safe because they are "a 'no-place'" (p. 313). I'm adding Pogue Harrison (1992) to Lacan, for a framework that is poetic and political rather than theoretical. Writing about the symbolism of the forest in art and literature as one such "no-place," Pogue Harrison spells out:

> If forests have typically been considered places of lawlessness, they have also provided havens for those who took up the cause of justice and fought the law's corruption. If they evoke associations of danger and abandon in our minds, they also evoke scenes of enchantment. In other words [...] the forest appears as a place where the logic of distinction goes astray. (Pogue Harrison, 1992, p. x)

This seems apt for academic development, where so often our workshops tackle changing practice, how to survive it, and how to stay true to yourself while doing so. Shakespearean forests, amongst the examples that Pogue Harrison uses, provide canonical models. I like the idea that academic development makes a wild space for both subversion and for holding to true values, and where distinctions break down a bit, so things are not so relentlessly geared for one discipline's epistemology nor for a single methodology of academic practice. That academic developers are oddly out of faculty seems to give us the same shadow of possibility that forests and marginal spaces give. I agree with Mark Johnson (1987, p. 140): "it is important to revive and enrich our notion of the imagination if we are to overcome certain undesirable effects of a deeply rooted set of dichotomies that have dominated western philosophy (e.g., body/mind, reason/imagination, science/art, cognition/emotion, fact/value...).". Academic development seminars can review these dichotomies, with a practical eye for how to teach differently in order to open taxonomies up for more variant possibilities. Nowhere are deeply rooted western assumptions more ubiquitous than in academia, where they may prove unhelpful to academic development. Like Geertsema and Laksov (2019, p. 2), I see it as critical to "locate academic development in the academic tradition, rather than as a service to be provided by institutional leadership," and like them, I see the potential for academic development to play "a brokering role that not only respects but honours diverse academic identities across disciplines and cultures." While frequently academic developers exist in "centres," and often are described as "central" because they are not situated within a faculty, the metaphor of margins, and perhaps forested margins, is as appropriate to academic development as the one of being central, and the two exist in a tension that is often relevant to our work. In a forest clearing...

Survival sits at the heart of this book's purpose. Academia seems beleaguered by an anxiety-driven audit culture, with a tightening fiscal squeeze. Too often we are awed by academia's demands, its rigour, and its elitist history. I argue we need to get over that and value who we are, beginning there with our self-development. Consider the fact that, as an academic, you are trained to lean towards criticality, and that, nonetheless, self-dissatisfaction can be an obstacle to achieving your best potential. Those of us who are working class bring fresh strengths. One book movingly and helpfully brings together academic women telling the stories of their working-class families and the awkwardness of acquiring a professional academic identity (Welsch, 2005). Reflection's power is demonstrated: a story recalling childhood shame at poverty is titled "You ain't ever gonna be better than me" and recognises the "unlikely gifts" that the author's mother gave her: the benefit of being an academic who is not "highbrow" acting or "uppity," so is able to make safe classrooms for students who recognise her as one of them (Brothe, 2005). There's an itinerary of admirable métiers. Parents took pride in a stalwart work ethic, and in fairness, recognising that "your ideals... are the most beautiful things you have" (Kendig, 2005, p. 7); "work ethic is important, attitude is crucial, and fair play and respect amongst workers is the golden rule". I recommend you read that book. It gives homely detail—academia can do with tribute to extramural realities. It demonstrates that you can draw on your own weaknesses for their affordances. Welsch's (2005) gallery of stories registers how valiant, intelligent and wise many working-class parents were—while basking in intellectual luxury, it is good to see that there are other values from humble roots that work very well in academia. Honan (2017, p. 22) entreats

> Join with me in this pleasurable work, engage passionately in ideas and ideals, find a joy that is productive. Relish the opportunities to demonstrate your foolish failures, revel in the ironic deconstructions of binds that tie us into the positions of compliance. Find the moments of pleasure within these confined spaces.

Recognising what is important to you—values, drivers, aversions and obsessions—helps you hold the ground for your own individuality and what that contributes. You can take pride in that mind wherein your life's experiences make you unique to contribute to this ambivalent space in which we work. The construction of a fruitcake imaginary celebrates the richness of your combination of lived and academic experiences.

For each of us, that experience is hectic. For eight years I developed a generic doctoral programme and became immersed in how challenging doctoral research and writing were for so many students. I felt an extraordinary privilege to be part of many heroic struggles. Struggle was not my own experience: I confess that doing a PhD suited me perfectly, in part because I was older, already with attitude, self-confidence and a keenness to partake of education. My sons had grown up and left home, so I no longer had to be anxious about my choices through need for an income that would sustain us as a family. I could chance my luck in the academic arena and if I failed to make it, well, it would be satisfying to have tried and reached the end of how far I could go. I had a Connaught Scholarship from the University of Toronto, and the luxury of my own project with institutional help pulling it together. This was so much more benign an environment that the unskilled work that I had undertaken, with low pay, sexism and scrutiny suggesting that our bosses thought we were doing something wrong and just hadn't caught us yet. I loved being a doctoral student, a conspicuous step up in status. What comes next is not fiction, nor autoethnography, but excerpts from an actual letter to my cousin written when I was in the first four months of my PhD, living in a Charles St student apartment in Toronto. Tucking in a letter about doctoral work within life felt justified because learning is always contextualised in life. Pauline aka Hunt kept and then, when she was tidying up years later, returned to me, a stack of such letters. The letters range from 1996 to 2000. They are undated, so it is only the content that gives clues as to when they were written. They have the feel of data for an article making the case that if you are a doctoral student you need to keep a sense of perspective on how academic work fits into life. This point is true for academics too.

Academia is a place of tension and of paradox. Inger Mewburn posted a blog whose core was speculation that "the university is a bad boyfriend; one day it's going to break your heart" (Mewburn, 2011, np). I'd agree that this is an apt analogy. The trouble is that I love my work, my university, my students, and so when changes are made that I regard as stupid, it's easy to find myself angry and hurt. Instead of wallowing around in grief, it seems better to look to the irony of institutional idiocy as funny. "You have to laugh" is said in my family (usually by my brother) about things that are not principally funny, but the suggestion is that laughing at life's irony is a better approach than remaining dismayed. An equal mixture of calm in the face of whatever confronts you, accompanied by a sense of humour, and an orientation towards pleasure are the doctoral attributes that I recommend.

* * *

Letter Home (December 1996), a Kind of Story

A bit more about my exams: the French one seemed miles easier than the passages we have worked on previously. In fact I may end up being grumpy because I just miss out passing, whereas Tanya, Wes and I were all quite content with the idea that none of us had a hope of passing this time round. Now we are optimistically thinking we may get around 60% and will be grouchy if it is 68 when we need 70… They were cute passages: one was about being able to detect drugs in hair and said that Peruvian mummies were found to have cocaine in their hair while Egyptian mummies had caffeine, tobacco and cannabis. Article finished with a nice little pun, based on the use of hair as evidence in court cases; "for the police, speech is silver, but the fleece is golden." The Latin likewise, which I have been putting a depressing amount of time into, seemed to make more sense than the last test…

Celebrated the sense of relief from mental burden by spring-cleaning the kitchen cupboards; everything in them removed to the living room floor. Had a Kali killing frenzy to cull any cockroaches that might be lurking in the recesses of the badly built cabinet unit—although my chemical attack did not bring out as many as I feared—and then washed everything down. I did not clean the top of the cupboards when we first got here on the basis that it was too disgusting, deeply sticky; I found it easier to pretend that it was some kind of fly-paper-like trap for cockroaches and should be left alone, but finally recuperated it, removing most of the paint in the process, and it will be a treat for Christmas to know that the areas where we do not look or touch but do keep the cake tins are no longer horror-movie wastelands. An utterly gross pastime requiring the rallying of all those Protestant ethics, British staunchness and even the Roman stoicism from Latin maxims, and in the end I left the last foot over the fridge…

Now have a large essay to write before Christmas on the Irish sovereignty hags—the work for it will later begin a difficult chapter of my thesis, in line with the two-birds-one-stone principle. I know that in the wonderful rare book collections in Toronto there is old Irish material, but need to find out what text I am looking for and whether it is available here. If I am lucky I will get just what I need and be able to come up with something legitimately able to be called "research." So far no luck, keep skimming through the annuls (*sic*?) flat out with narry a hag to be found…

I have also now had my thesis proposal accepted officially and been given a committee, one of whom is a woman I have never heard of, so I should go and introduce myself over the next few days too. She wrote a great swathe of criticism on my proposal, so I had a bit of a sinking feeling. Some of it was completely valid, but some of it I don't agree with—she seems to think humour and colloquialism have no place in academic writing—I strongly disagree and loathe the boredom of more of that dreary old relentlessly academic tone. But my lovely supervisor said that she had seen the "mainly nugatory" remarks, but had also talked to the woman and decided she was just trying to sweep clean as a new broom at Toronto, and was not going to be a problem, but wanted to help. (Yes, of course I had to look nugatory up in the dictionary; it means trifling, worthless, futile, not valid)…

I am finally succumbing to the idea that my high blood pressure will need medication. Had an echo scan on my heart, which I found unnerving because of the horrid surging noises it seemed to be making, like a volcano under the ocean, only miles more gross since it was not actually that but a body. Also had my kidneys ultrasound-scanned a few weeks ago, and then had to carefully collect all pee for 24 hours, which gave me a happy sense of productivity and usefulness…

We went dancing with the other grad students at a Latin American gay dance hall on Friday night. There were the perfectly straight couples displaying their perfect renditions of Latin American dancing/simulated sexual acts while the transvestites elegantly posed displaying perfect renditions of '50s femininity. We bungled round energetically and got sweaty…

Babysat last night and Zoe who is two woke up and cried. Her parents had said if she wakes up just leave her, she will go back to sleep (and she is suspicious of me), but after about a quarter of an hour with her frustration that mummy wasn't coming getting more and more indignant, and the volume rising, and she shares a room with her sister who slept through the racket, I went in and picked her up and took her into her mum's room to say, would you be happier sleeping in mummy's bed till she gets home? But no, Zoe slid off the bed, and went and checked the living room, which had not mummy and daddy in it, but Blackie watching tellie, and she gave a few more despairing sobs, indicated that she wanted to get back in her cot, and shut up and went to sleep like a sensible little girl. Phew!

Have a big stack of books for this essay which is nonetheless feeling still-born with no primary material to date, just heaps of tangential stuff… But exams are over! Love, Sue

* * *

Choose the adjectives and accompanying adverbs that you want to be known by.

As an academic, teacher, researcher, administrator, facilitator, I most want to be

lucid; ethical; inspiring; knowledgeable; fun; witty; cutting edge; solid; reliable; provocative; stylish; caring; homely; colourful; deep level; rigorous; relaxed; authentically myself; beyond and above myself; internationally situated; methodologically appropriate; resistant to discipline strictures; resistant to social bias; resistant to academic pedantry; challenging; demanding; flexible; humble; community-focused; wide-ranging; eclectic; playful; artistic; artisanal… you could pick from these and add others that are important to you.

Adverbs that I'd like others to attach to my adjectives include

extremely; cautiously; provocatively; reassuringly; startlingly; surprisingly; and wonderfully.

Itemise three small steps towards the academic you want to be. Block off calendar time to take these steps. Write a section in your annual reporting or promotion document, e.g., "Wanting to be more challenging in my teaching, I…"; "Aiming to contribute to making the university more welcoming for international students, I…"; "Needing to step into an international arena with my research, I…."

To be continued, by you rather than by me…

Try a self-audit exercise for yourself on what matters and doesn't matter, what irritates, and what inspires. Start by looking inward. **What values do you bring with you to your career?**

- From your family and upbringing (or in resistance to them)?
- From your experience?
- From stories, films, music, art…?
- From cultural or religious belief?
- From education?
- From times when people hurt you, or times when they saved you and warmed your heart?
- From looking at people you really admire?

What else? Add to this list of prompts seeking to surface values from the core of your being so that the exercise becomes your own, one you can adapt to different teaching situations.

References

Acker, S., & Armenti, C. (2004). Sleepless in academia. *Gender and Education, 16*(1), 4–24.

Ahmed, S., & Stacey, J. (2001a). Introduction: Dermographics. In S. Ahmed & J. Stacey (Eds.), *Thinking through the skin* (pp. 1–17). New York, NY: Routledge.

Ahmed, S., & Stacey, J. (2001b). *Thinking through the skin.* London, UK: Routledge.

Aitchison, C., Catterall, J., Ross, P. I., & Burgin, S. (2012). "Tough love and tears": Learning doctoral writing in the sciences. *Higher Education Research & Development, 31*(4), 435–447.

Aitchison, C., & Lee, A. (2006). Research writing: Problems and pedagogies. *Teaching in Higher Education, 11*(3), 265–278.

Atkinson, N. (2005). The ever present past. In K. A. Welsch (Ed.), *Those winter Sundays: Female academics and their working class parents* (pp. 84–92). Lanham, MD: University of America Press.

Badenhorst, C., & Guerin, C. (2016). *Research literacies and writing pedagogies for masters and doctoral writers.* Leiden, The Netherlands: Studies in Writing Series, Brill.

Becher, T., & Trowler, P. (2001). *Academic tribes and territories: Intellectual enquiry and the culture of disciplines* (2nd ed.). Philadelphia, PA: Open University Press.

Berg, M., & Seeber, B. M. (2017). *The slow professor: Challenging the culture of speed in the academy.* Toronto, ONT: University of Toronto Press.

Brailsford, I. (2011). "The ha'porth of tar to save the ships": Student counselling and vulnerable university students. *History of Education, 40*(3), 357–370.

Brothe, C. (2005). You ain't ever gonna be better than me. In K. A. Welsch (Ed.), *Those winter Sundays: Female academics talk about their working class Parents* (pp. 13–20). Lanham, MD: University Press of America.

Brown, L., & Watson, P. (2010). Understanding the experience of female doctoral students. *Journal of Further and Higher Education, 34*(3), 385–404.

Cantwell, R., & Scevak, J. (2010). *An academic life: A handbook for new academics.* Camberwell, UK: ACER.

Carter, S. (2008). Examining the doctoral thesis: A discussion. *Innovations in Education and Teaching International, 45*(4), 365–374.

Carter, S. (2014). The methodology of magpies. *International Journal of Research & Method in Education, 37*(2), 125–136.

Carter, S., Blumenstein, M., & Cook, C. (2013). Different for women?: The challenges of doctoral study. *Teaching in Higher Education, 18*(4), 339–351.

Carter, S., & Laurs, D. (Eds.). (2014). *Developing Generic Support for Doctoral Students: Practice and Pedagogy.* London/New York: Routledge.

Carter, S., Laurs, D., Chant, L., & Wolgramm-Foliaki, E. (2017b). Indigenous knowledge and supervision: Changing the lens. *Innovations in Education and Teaching International, 55*(3), 384–393. https://doi.org/10.1080/14703297.2017.1403941

Debowski, S. (2012). *The new academic: A strategic handbook.* New York, NY: Open University Press.

Finke, L. A. (1992). *Feminist theory, women's writing.* Ithaca, NY: Cornell University Press.

Flavell, J. H. (1979). Metacognition and cognitive monitoring: A new area of cognitive-developmental Inquiry. *American Psychologist, 34*(10), 906–911.

Garrett, G., & Davies, G. (2010). *Herding cats: Being advice to aspiring academic and research leaders.* Axminster, UK: Triarchy Press.

Geertsema, J., & Laksov, K. B. (2019). Turning challenges into opportunities: (Re-)vitalizing the role of academic development. *International Journal for Academic Development, 24*(1), 1–6.

Golding, C. (2013). Must we gather data? A place for the philosophical study of higher education. *Higher Education Research Development, 32*(1), 152–155.

Grant, B., & Barrow, M. (2013). Fashioning docile teacher bodies? The strange space of the "staff teaching seminar". *International Journal for Academic Development, 18*(4), 306–317.

Hau'ofa, E. (2008). *We are the ocean: Selected works.* Honolulu, HA: University of Haiwai'i Press.

Honan, E. (2017). Producing moments of pleasure within the confines of the Neoliberal University. In S. Riddle, M. K. Harmes, & P. A. Danaher (Eds.), *Producing pleasure in the Contemporary University* (pp. 13–24). Rotterdam/Boston/Taipei: Sense.

hooks, b. (1991). Theory as liberatory practice. *Yale Journal of Feminism and Law, 4*(1), 1–13.

Johnson, M. (1987). *The body in the mind: The bodily basis of meaning, imagination and reason.* Chicago, IL: University of Chicago Press.

Kendig, D. (2005). The seams that stood all the changes: Keeping it together in academia. In K. A. Welsch (Ed.), *Those winter Sundays: Female academics and their working class parents* (pp. 1–12). Lanham, MD: University Press of America.

Kirby, V. (1994). Response to Jane Gallop's "The Teacher's Breasts": Bad form. In J. J. Matthews (Ed.), *Jane Gallop seminar papers: Proceedings of the Jane Gallop Seminar and public lecture "The Teacher's Breasts"* (pp. 17–22). Canberra, ACT: Humanities Research Centre.

Manathunga, C. (2007). "Unhomely" academic developer identities: More post-colonial explorations. *International Journal for Academic Development, 12*(1), 25–34.

Mewburn, I. (2011). Is the university a bad boyfriend? Retrieved from https://thesiswhisperer.com/2011/08/09/is-the-university-a-bad-boyfriend/

Negus, K., & Pickering, M. (2004). *Creativity, communication and cultural value*. London, UK: Sage.

Pogue Harrison, R. (1992). *Forests: The shadow of civilization*. Chicago, IL: Chicago University Press.

Samuels, L. (2002). Relinquish intellectual property. *New Literary History, 33*(2), 357–374.

Sutton, P. (2014). A paradoxical academic identity: Fate, utopia and hope. *Teaching in Higher Education, 20*(1), 37–47. https://doi.org/10.1080/13562517.2014.957265

Swartz, P. C. (2005). "A circle" or, strangely, a life in school. In K. A. Welsch (Ed.), *Those winter Sundays: Female academics and their working class parents* (pp. 69–83). Lanham, MD: University of America Press.

Theodore, R., Tustin, K., Kiro, C., Gollop, M., Taumoepeau, M., Taylor, N., et al. (2016). Māori university graduates: Indigenous participation in higher education. *Higher Education Research and Development, 38*(3), 604–618.

Tolkien, J. R. R. (2001). *The Lord of the Rings*. Boston, MA: Houghton Mifflin.

Webber, M. (2009). The multiple selves and realities of a Māori researcher. *Māori and Indigenous Review, 1*, 1–8.

Welsch, K. A. (Ed.). (2005). *Those winter Sundays: Female academics and their working class parents*. Lanham, MD: University Press of America.

Zandy, J. (2005). Foreword. In K. A. Welsch (Ed.), *Those winter Sundays: Female academics and their working class parents*. Lanham, MD: University Press of America.

CHAPTER 4

Teaching, Research, Service, Self

Abstract This chapter homes in on the different arenas of academic work: teaching, research and service. It considers academic citizenship and professionalism. Acknowledging the messy reality that considerable academic work is invisible from audit scrutiny, it directly confronts some of the bothersome ironies of academia, such as when funding cuts run counter to institutional rhetoric suggesting socially responsible values. The chapter moves to consider how, amongst this mixed work environment, academics might find ways to advance the educational and social causes that matter to them. This chapter's story about a winter afternoon sports field shows different approaches to making the most of the habitus. The chapter concludes with emphasis on the personal, and on individual, maintenance of ethical values.

Keywords Teaching review • Theories of teaching and learning • Research writing • Academic service • Academic citizenship • Academic professionalism

The academic career generally occurs over three intertwined zones of work: teaching, research and service. This chapter critiques the professional reality of these three arenas, starting with teaching, considering research writing, then service, and then the work we all do that is often invisible, the informal mentoring, the writing that doesn't make it to

S. Carter, *Academic Identity and the Place of Stories*,
https://doi.org/10.1007/978-3-030-43601-8_4

publication, the invisible labour of consultation, care and support. Some of the book's earlier recommendations about seeing the funny side of irony, stretching imagination and drawing on core identity may help both with practice and with reporting on practice.

Work across these entwined and entangled demands occurs in an environment in which "there is usually no culture of uniformity… [and] there is a place for guile and political acumen" (Garret & Davies, 2010, p. 1). This assessment of academia is right. It is politically astute to quell suspicion of student assessment as being affected by perceived leniency in grading, or popularity rather than by quality teaching. Then, it is fairly common to want to publish from funded research on some aspect that the funders aren't interested in, and to need to manipulate time to ensure that publications meet funders' expectations without your own research profile becoming skewed away from your own interests. Somehow we balance contingencies as part of our developing professionalism: "guile" is such a negative word and, arguably, "political acumen" can be read fairly negatively too. But we can develop acumen for surviving amongst the slippage of academic work. It's like developing strategies for playing a game.

Teaching

How did you learn to teach? Were you initially nervous? Did you spend way too much time preparing each lecture because you were terrified of being seen as not the real thing? As a petrified novice, I watched other middle-aged women who were experienced lecturers as possible models, because I knew that I needed a persona I could perform out of *my* body with all the cultural baggage that middle-aged femininity entails. Being a middle-aged female academic seemed to require avoiding being mistaken for a generic mum who might raise grades if pestered, or make other concessions. I watched female experts who showed their prowess in ways that were within my reach. Novice teachers build personae that fit and work. As much as I admired the energetic engineer who rides a unicycle across the lecture theatre, piggybacking a student who is juggling three balls (AkldUni4Schools, 2010), that was never an option for me. Learning advisor work has taught me that most new academics feel nervous about how they, with their body, their way of speaking and their cultural background, will be seen as a teacher. We academics are easily troubled that students won't like us, and won't learn from us. We can be gnawed at by self-doubt that drives us to spend way too much time paying attention to all the wrong things. I would like to think about ways to turn that self-doubt around so that we each draw on our sparky innovative imaginations, and on our particular quirks of body, voice and culture. At the same time as we construct those identities, we can take opportunities to learn from other teachers.

In my current job to 2020, I have routinely observed others' teaching in order to give advice (Bell & Cooper, 2013) until I put the material for teaching review into order and accessibility, with advice on how to review teaching constructively (Siddiqui, Jonas-Dwyer, & Carr, 2007). Now, we encourage academics to peer review, aware of how much is to be learned by watching others teach (Bernstein, 2008), and how energising it is to talk to workmates about teaching (Cosh, 1998). Reviewing teaching, you are present in the class not for the content of the lecture, nor for the meta-cognitive learning when you can see how the discipline thinks and talks, but to notice how teaching for learning occurs. Academic developers benefit from learning about disciplinary preferences—and usually the content of lectures is interesting too. Primarily, though, you are focused on teaching and learning, watching for how that magic is brought about through the curriculum design, the teacher's presence and persona, her pacing and use of time and tempo. I've been curious as to why some lecturers can set an in-class exercise and students do it, for the most, and other lecturers get no response to the same strategy: students wait out the five minutes attending to other digital business (online purchases, Facebook, etc.) until they are given the answer. I've wondered what combinations of innovation and teaching persona cause real engagement. Any teacher who sets an in-class exercise can be said to be "teaching for student engagement," but some achieve *engagement* with that ploy and others fail to.

Perhaps, too, "student engagement" is a metaphor that has lost its grunt. "Student engagement" has a root meaning that can be taken freshly again to mean a committed connection with the topic being studied. When that happens, it is exhilarating. The term "leadership" is another metaphor jaundiced by overuse. It is part of the reporting lexicon at my institution–we are asked to demonstrate how we show leadership in teaching, research and service. Many of us dislike reporting on our performance at all because the compulsion that we do so implies that we are not trusted, and because reporting takes time away from activities that seem more important. We seem to be assumed to be ineffective until we prove otherwise and it takes considerable unproductive time gathering evidence. So we can become jaundiced to words like student engagement and leadership, the language of self-reporting. Both terms gesture to something marvellous, however; is it possible to suspend disbelief in their common coinage and take heart from them again? Studying early English literature requires such a suspension of cynicism. Leadership comes through, raw and inspiring, in warrior epics. Reading *Beowulf* to be captivated requires ignoring all the subsequent derivatives to find the force of the original root meaning. Then, it's inspiring, and moving, a model of leadership as perseverance despite overwhelming odds. Note to self: remember to suspend perfectly logical cynicism about over-used institutional jargon and to stay enchanted by teaching and learning.

Teachers who care about real engagement try different means to achieve it, on an endless quest to shift learners forward through hard learning. Good teaching and learning take effort, design and creativity on multiple levels. I speculate that firing up students' imaginations may depend on a myriad of cultural and social cues in the class or the digital teaching medium as well as on professional care with curriculum development. Amanda Bill describes creativity as "an achievement sustained through the production and repetition of many small acts and signs made significant through particular social and cultural categories" (Bill, 2017, p. 249). Perhaps learning is enabled when students recognise and respond to a teacher's exploitation of social and cultural capital as they license their imagination in creativity. Theory prompted by the shift from face-to-face to digital teaching teases out aspects of learning with attention to social aspects of cognitive engagement. Attempts to understand this transition began with a "community of inquiry" model (Garrison, Anderson & Archer, 2000) that identified social presence, cognitive presence and teacher presence as working together to ensure that real learning happens in the digital world. "Social presence," and emotional presence (Cleveland-Innes & Campbell, 2012) resonate with the need for academics to fire up their social and emotional projections as teachers. Professionalism demands consideration of assessment based on intended learning outcomes, but teaching and learning also require cognitive sparks that catch. I'm suggesting that the teacher's use of imagination taps cultural capital (perhaps organically) rather than being only rationally intentional.

When reviewing teaching, I have sometimes noticed the performance of recognisable literary tropes, the magus, the fool, the warrior, the maiden, big sister or wise old woman: as teachers we can choose to be "creators of our identities… in the expressive form we give to them" (Negus & Pickering, 2004, p. 34). There're so many variables affecting teaching and learning—self-regulation has been added to Garrison et al.'s community of practice model (Shea &Bidjerano, 2009). Educational theories are useful because they equip teachers with a quasi-scientific language for reporting that their teaching is research-informed and that it's positioned theoretically. Bean-counters who evaluate respond favourably to the appearance of quasi-science. I argue, though, that this approach, without awareness of the magic of teaching and learning, blunts the potential that education has to prompt holistic growth, that is, growth towards wisdom, the acquiring of metacognitive experience, self-knowledge and self-appreciation. Although theories offer something valuable, they don't account for what happens in practice when learners change as to who and how they are. Education is an art, with art's potential to inspire.

So what are the limitations of education theory? It is a commonplace in education discourse to disparage the cranky old "sage on the stage" in favour of the seemingly more servile, student-focused "guide on the side." It's more complex than that: any way of teaching can work well or less well. As an undergraduate student, a newcomer to academia, I was drawn into wanting to stay within academia by the cognitive performance of those sages on the stage. In literature studies, they could begin their intellectual gymnastics with textual interpretation, and take a twirl through historical contexts, contemporary literature, critical readings, etymologies of key words, and they performed the text, bringing it to life, all the while flicking out ideas with potential for more study, and opportunities for countering arguments to their own. In retrospect, literature studies is one discipline that is unashamed about drawing on the imagination, and is rich because of that. To my mind the educational theories that frame my work as an academic developer are the weaker for their quasi-scientific leanings if teachers feel that citing theory and following practice from the latest jargon terms are all you need.

Taxonomies of learning that categorise how it works never quite account for the chaos and interconnectivity of the imagination. Bloom's taxonomy (e.g., Bloom, 1965) appeals perhaps for its geometry, and because it allows teachers to show how their class design and curriculum are based on a recognised model that, again, makes teaching look like a science. In my experience, though, learners don't step tidily from one level to another. The terms on Bloom's taxonomy name aspects of learning;

what would happen if the terms were delivered in a poem rather than a table? I'm proposing the result might be more truthful to what happens, even though I am aware that a poem will not work as readily to support evidence of good teaching for promotion. We need the quasi-scientific presentation for a neoliberal environment. We can both use it and recognise its limitations, remembering to stay amused by the irony of managing magic within an accounting system.

"Deep-level learning" is an aspirational phrase with its metaphor of learning that affects the core. Yet deep and surface learning (Marton & Saljo, 1976) ought to be allies rather than opposites, because surface learning is part of deep learning. Surface-level learning is commonly understood as the result of note-taking when those sages take to the stage, assumed to be transmitting facts rather than magic. The facts are then rote-learned for giving back in tests. Yet memory has a role to play, because internalisation fuels cognition. Internalisation of foundational facts in any discipline feeds the imagination, and is part of becoming and being. In an age when information is so readily accessible, it seems as though there really is little need to learn facts, although often disciplines have foundational premises that need to be internalised before you can *become* a practitioner in a discipline, a sociologist or engineer, say. Some of what must be understood include threshold concepts that are troublesome, hard to grasp and internalise (Meyer & Land, 2005). From back when teaching and learning were within church auspices (funded and audited by the church rather than by neoliberal accountants), the west had a pedagogic belief that, only through remembering information, could we develop spiritually. Further, "as an *art*, memory was most importantly associated in the Middle Ages with composition, not simply with retention" (Carruthers and Ziolkowski, 2002, p. 3, my italics). Mary Carruthers explains that, for almost two thousand years, memory was linked metaphorically to the heart and the "vital spirit": the Latin verb for recollect, *recordari*, means to bring back to the heart; Old English *herte* was where thoughts occurred (Carruthers, 1990, p. 48). Augustine (354–430), for example, locates memory as the habitat of God, declaring gratitude that "Thou has given this honour to my memory to reside in it… For in thinking on Thee, I have passed beyond such part of it as the beasts also have, for I found Thee not among the images of corporeal things…" (cited in Carruthers, 1990, pp. 48–49). It has been said that Asian learning cultures favour rote or revisional learning, i.e., surface-level learning, which makes for a cultural divide when international students encounter the demand for engagement (Watkins & Biggs, 1996). Westerners seem to have lost cultural awareness that memory's scrupulous internalisation belongs amongst identity development.

Educational theories are helpful, all part of my repertoire as an academic developer who gives advice on preparing teaching portfolios. But I want academic development to locate the heart and soul of teaching and learning. That takes art's creativity and belief in inspiration rather than, or in addition to, science's objectivity and propensity to be countable. Pulling the Augustine quotation up as an example that western theories once linked memory to the spiritual aspect of learning, I see that in mentioning memory's "images of corporeal things," Augustine seems to be aware that memory, like metaphor, and like new materialism's thinking through the skin, combines body, mind and soul, or its secular equivalent, inner core. Augustine aspires towards the divine, but recognises the body as foundational. Of course theories that help teaching and learning need to be given respect. But theories scratch at the sides of something complex, where imagination plays a role that cannot be readily nailed down.

Could we factor in the role of imagination for teaching success, and awareness that, as teachers, we want to fire up learners' imaginations? Flipped classrooms attempt this, and Scholarship of Teaching and Learning discourse considers whether and how it works, the quite radical reversal of teaching and learning, with more onus on students themselves to learn the basics and with the classroom space transformed to active performance of what can be done in the discipline. Experimenting with class design lets us chase down the idea that "[t]he learning self is a moving self, in a dynamic relationship with knowledge" (Kamler & Thomson, 2006, p. 18). There's more to this than setting measurable learning outcomes…

Research

Research methods vary considerably across disciplines. Research writing does too, in alignment with different epistemologies. Always, though, academic writing is bothersome, demanding accuracy for clarity, calling up emotions because it matters, and it matters because the writer's identity is constructed within their prose. I found, from surveying 226 accredited supervisor, that there was no numerically significant difference in supervisory challenges when participants taught and supported doctoral writing (Carter, Kensington-Miller, & Courtney, 2017). Research writing and its review operate in a sphere that is "often dependent on tacit knowledge, with its own ritualized practices and mythologies" (Aitchison & Guerin, 2014, p. 53); all who seek to establish themselves in this sphere must satisfy their particular disciplinary tribe (Becher & Trowler, 2001), yet the experiences of tribal initiation and ongoing compliance are somehow quite similar across disciplines. The fact that text signifies authorial identity makes word choice matter and rejection painful. While especially challenging for fledgling researchers (Aitchison et al., 2012; Aitchison & Lee, 2006), it tests seasoned academics too: my centre hosts academic writing support that gets good uptake each semester by academics who find sharing their frustration in collegial writing groups and writing in the company of other writers help with productivity (Aitchison & Guerin, 2014).

Writing groups provide a time and a place, so that writing becomes timetabled, like teaching and meetings (Kensington-Miller & Carter, 2019). They make safe spaces where we can laugh together at pedantry (Thesen, 2014), releasing the tension of anxiety and subduing the sense of inadequacy. Without the compulsion provided by a group framework, writing fits in around other aspects of work and life, often being what is dropped when the pressure is on. Yet the authorial identity that the act of writing pulls into being gives another element of intrigue for those of us who like words.

Authorial identity becomes a significant aspect of who we are, another area where imagination and creativity can be brought into play. That sounds easy, and it is not easy. Research writing is frustrating and time-greedy. Rejection is demoralising and angering. Successful writers have written on how they manage this, demonstrating authorial expertise as they do so—these books are worth reading for pleasure as well as motivation. Annie Lamott pulls a comedic approach from the negative emotions that occur around writing, her murderous feelings toward rejecting reviewers, and her suicidal thoughts filled with self-loathing, while showing a dialogue between writing expertise and expertise for handling the hard aspects of life (Lamott, 1995). She declares, "To be a good writer, you not only have to write a great deal but you have to care. You do not have to have a complicated moral philosophy. But a writer always tries, I think, to be part of the solution…" (Lamott, 1995, p. 107). And she gives a very concrete description of writing in response to being asked how to write:

> You try to sit down at approximately the same time every day. This is how you train your unconscious to kick in for you creatively. So you sit down at, say, nine every morning or ten every night. … you turn on your computer

and bring up the right file, and then you stare at it for an hour or so. You begin rocking, just a little at first, and then like a huge autistic child… and you try to quiet your mind… (Lamott, 1995, p. 6)

Helen Sword has academic writing as her area of research expertise. Usually, when you read published work, you do not see all the labour that has gone into producing that clean, stylish prose, but the following sentence gives a back-room view of the writer at work:

However, I found that I could seldom even get to the end of a sentence without retracing my steps to make some small change along the way—in this one, for example, I've just gone back to replace "*before* retracing my steps" with "*without* replacing my steps"; and after that I went back to replace "this *sentence*" with "this *one*"; and then I replaced "*and then*" with "*after that*"—and now I'm reluctant to come to the end of (no, better to say, "I'm reluctant to *place the final period at* the end of") this sentence because I promised myself that I wouldn't tinker with it any more after—oh no, now I've just realised that "*the final period*" would work better as the final thump, so I'd better try again: and now I'm reluctant to come to the end of this sentence because I promised myself that I wouldn't tinker with it any more after placing the final period. (Sword, 2017, pp. 59–60)

Her sentence captures perfectly the sense of an artisan at work, pausing and pondering, and bothering to take time towards a stylish, well-polished product. The sentence suggests how long it can take to write well, and yet it also somehow catches a sense of the pleasure of crafting.

Academics should learn how to savour writerly pleasure while remembering that writing is part of business: upskilling there is a worthwhile part of professionalism. Stephen King describes fitting writing-as-a-living into his life, emphasising that it is just work. King discards the idea of a classical muse for the man in the basement who keeps the furnace going (S. King, 2000, pp. 163–164):

He's a basement guy. You have to descend to his level, and once you get down there… you have to do all the grunt labour… while the muse sits and smokes cigars and admires his bowling trophies and pretends to ignore you. Do you think this is fair? I think it's fair…

King insists that it's fair because writing is just a job, a bit like a labourer's job, something that earns you the living you want, the beers that you might drink while you work at writing. While academics bemoan the pressure of an audit culture, King's workerly approach focuses on the sharper reality of paying for groceries. Academic Paul Silvia is similarly down to earth. He advises putting the "'inner writer' back on its leash and muzzl[ing] it… [while releasing] the 'outer writer' who is productively outer facing" (Silvia, 2010, p. 3).

Academic writing's construction of identity has long interested me as to how it plays out in terms of self-knowledge. Writing is both an artistic expression of self and an appeal to the epistemological tribe for ongoing acceptance, with each article or book reconstructing, renegotiating and reconsidering. Research writing is a symbolic act. Rolling in Lacan's Name of the Father, a noumena of the figure who holds authority, I've admitted that

> as an academic woman, I find it satisfying to inhabit the symbolic role of the Name of the Father,… able to appropriate the qualities of a traditionally masculine way of talking – rigorous academic writing – when it enhances my creation. … Voice [in arts and humanities research writing] relates to subjectivity but is constructed, too, shrewdly, and possibly with style in mind. (Carter, 2012, p. 415)

The textual identity that inhabits research writing can be understood through theories on gender and power. Now I'm threading academic writing into theories of metaphor and imagination, where all those facets of life experience, including gender, and with nuances from so many other identity markers, can contribute to research creativity. Here's a speculation: if metaphors are founded on physical experience that gives a means to cognitive complexity, and if they can then be stretched to reach, always futilely, towards the sublime, language is a medium where body, mind and soul (or inner core being) struggle together to make meaning of original knowledge or understanding. Academics who need to publish their research probably don't feel in quest of epiphany, but do grapple somewhat heroically towards meaning-making. It is hard work. Academic writing is bothersome.

Those who feel bothered by the need to choose style and degree of creativity as they fit words together could try to see writing as one of their academic craft skills, within their academic calling. I argue that it aligns with teaching in that research writing also makes new knowledge available, new to the world and not just the learner in your class, and yet still an act of teaching and learning with colleagues who are interested in the same area. The entire academic career makes the world a little better, through the combined efforts of particular imaginations speaking to each other, connecting, and taking things further. That last sentence is so out in the wastelands beyond the reach of criticality, out in the thickets where blessings get counted. Sometimes, though, I feel that working always critically makes it hard for us to see how privileged we are and how rich that privilege is.

Service

"Service" in the academic contract is often interpreted as administration, seen as a burden, and resented as a distraction from teaching and research (MacFarlane, 2007, p. 63). Even worse, perhaps, it can be seen as customer service, when students are considered the customers of the neoliberal university-as-business (MacFarlane, 2007, p. 64). They expect degrees because they have paid fees for them. One of MacFarlane's academic participants linked academic service with "the service industries" (p. 65)—work a bit like cleaning the rooms in a hotel or waiting at tables. Yet, MacFarlane gathered more positive comparisons, with academic service as something like community service. Community service can refer to a term handed down in courts as punishment, but serving a community has the possibility of making a difference for the better in other people's lives. That is worth doing. As academics, we have the opportunity. We get paid pretty well to do it.

Perhaps the strongest service results from inspection of your own values and pleasures. Which group/s within academia do you want to help? What about out there in the world—are there causes where your academic expertise would lend weight to progress, to restraint, to improvement? Again, the strong indigenous sense of family and community lends exemplars that might help a shift in attitude, from antipathy to service to the same kind of feeling we have with family responsibilities… that it matters and we'll feel better if we do it.

I've mentioned already that this book was written as I taught ACADPRAC 702, that conversations in that class were primarily around academic service, and that this prompted me to want to write on how to develop happily as an academic using imagination as the driver, pleasure as the compass and your own values as the road map. In that course, one academic chose to champion the provision of unisex toilets as more comfortable for transgender people. The practical work of their assignment entailed an audit of all the toilets on campus, locating where there already were unisex ones, and a formal request, backed by literature, facts and logic, that a few more toilets be changed to unisex in the interest of equity, with instruction as to where these needed to be. The written assignment was a personal story, with literature showing why transgender students needed to be considered as an equity responsibility. Another 702 student produced a guide for field trips, concerned that the alcohol consumption that produced bonding also isolated some cultural groups, and wanting to ensure that all students felt comfortable and included in the social warmth of the trip. Then one tidied up an impossibly cluttered, disorganised laboratory, establishing an inventory and sign-out system; another decorated the staff space so that it was homely; and two worked together to establish a community of practice for academics on teaching-only contracts. All worked on things that improved their environment. The course let us also work together at the language for annual reporting to label these activities acts of leadership.

As you audit yourself throughout this book, can you tie the different components of your professional and personal selves together in a way that makes sense of your life? Can you find yourself in there? You could read accounts of academic life that are certainly likely to resonate. Frances Kelly (2015: 1153) describes a day in the life of an academic. She begins by postulating that "the university lives (partly) in the imagination, in the ideas, sentiments, values and beliefs that individuals hold in relation to the university"; that individual thoughts create the university, or multiple universities; and that we embody the university. She writes as "an individual self in the university who thinks and analyses, uses her imagination, has memories, hopes and dreams, eats and drinks" (p. 1153). Andrew Sparkes (2007) tells a story of academic pressure that was threatening his health, while the music of Leonard Cohen, and especially Cohen's lyrics, kept him sane. At the end of that article, what he is left with is certainty of how much music matters to him, how loyal his wife is, how empathetic his colleagues are, and how much other academics suck up his story thirstily for talking about the life as it really is (Sparkes, 2007). Sparkes (2007) is responding to Ronald J. Pelias (2004), who grappled down a book on "academic and daily life." Pelias recounted his backstory, which included dropping out, then dropping back in, but being drafted to the invasion of Vietnam before finishing his master's degree (Pelias, 2004). One chapter recounts a day in the life of an academic (Kelly, 2015 riffed from this structural method of social critique), noting each point when critical judgement affects people (pp. 111–121). Pelias (2004, p. 113) starts with the D he gives to an ungrammatical essay "without thinking of the racism, classism and sexism of academic standards and without celebrating that the student claims a deep affinity for a poem." Then a colleague comes in enraged by the reviewers' comments about his article, showing that it is not only poor, illiterate students who are hurt by critical harshness: we all are. "Everyone is caught in the same critical grind, giving out and taking in comments designed to say how we are positioned, rated, ranked." Both Sparkes, and more so Pelias, were seeking a heart that might thump in academia with more vitality than a rigorous accounting system. Pelias concludes with a chapter titled "What the heart learns." Where I include short stories in this book, Pelias, engaged in a very similar task, includes poems in his. He finishes with "a cautious belief in the promise of connection" (Pelias, 2004, p. 172), perhaps pleased, like so many of us, with connection with others, with ideas, and with others in thinking through ideas. Where Sparkes took life from music, Pelias, a poet, draws back to the power of poetry to make sense of the academic life:

> The heart learns that poems are the hypotheses that let our hearts pump, love and forgive… We may grind against ourselves, unskilled in locating healing comparisons. Poems, though, give our hearts permission and hope. They are open promises, waiting. (2004, p. 172)

That we are paid in a job to contribute to making the institution and perhaps society and maybe even the world a better place is something to keep in mind as a privilege despite all that is ironic and wrong about aspects of academia.

* * *

Finding the Field…

In some ways, this is the field's story. You could say a sort of epistemology if you were that way inclined. Seasons in and out. Now, it is winter, a dull grey afternoon. The busy season. Two teams are settling into the second half of the game. The seniors A and B teams trying each other on. There's room to swap some of the boys round if they show their form.

The Crockly boys are there, three brothers, Kevin, Bradley and Bunter. Bunter's the youngest but the biggest of the three. These lads are big of bone and brawn, fast and fearless, swift-stepping and side-swiping, duckers and dodgers, hard-handed and high hoofers and loud in the bar besides. Irish backgrounds, and legends in their own small time and place. They grizzle about each other but they can read each other too and slot in together to get some good action going.

Bunter is being rucked in the head at the bottom of a small heap of bodies. His mum screams abuse from the sideline, growing more foul and imaginative with each expletive phrase. Later Brad will explain to her that you have to ruck someone who is holding onto the ball on the ground. They've got to let it go. It's got to be done. Bunter knows that. He was just trying it on. He got rucked and he knows that is fair enough. To be honest, she's a bit of an embarrassment, mum, not that it matters.

One small girl stamps through a puddle some distance from the string of spectators, away from where mummy is. The puddle is not too deep, but agreeably big. She's laughing, absorbed. And she's joined by three other small kids, who follow her back and forth through the puddle, giggling and whooping, shoving a bit, stamping to splash themselves and each other. Humans like rituals involving water. They like group work, cranking up the tempo, seeing how far they're going to go.

It's the wee girl in a layered pink fairy frock, gumboots and puffer jacket who first slides right over, skids along covered in mud and water, and hysterical with the pleasure of something happening. She's the leader. She's staked out a new depth to this game. Soon all the children are muddy all over. It is terrific fun.

When Kevin boots the ball out for a corner line-out, and it bounces off further than it should in that direction, one parent spots the kids. Groans and grunty laughter run along the sideline. Look at those kids. Might as well leave them. Little bastards. Get them in the shower when we get home.

Bradley takes the kick and converts.

At the far end of the sports ground field, the din of the game is just a rise and fall, like faded wallpaper if wallpaper could sing and if you thought about it. A ditch runs through, surrounded by plants, including nasturtiums. Natalie is seated on a folding stool drawing a leaf in detail. She has the shape of other leaves around it, but this one she wants to capture precisely. She moves to delineate each delicate vein. It is slow work, likely to take several hours. There is nothing special about this leaf, which is why it matters.

And really it is cold for this exercise, but detailed pencil drawing is how she restores herself. Mindfulness, not on her own body, skin, toes, and where your nails join on, but on the tender random beauty of the world around her, the smallness of perfection. Her own body slowly disappears into the gentle breathing of the nasturtiums. She has learned how to do this and it is what she likes to do when she can. This is a meditation that her soul needs.

Kevin is heading for the line, side-stepping and stepping on the gas. He's bleeding from the head when he comes out of the tackle, but handsomely so. Good boy. There's a scrum, and it is Colin who gets the ball over. This is a darned good game, actually. Nice highlight of the weekend.

A rim of houses edge the field, ex-state houses, solid, squat. In each house, there are people with their own grey-afternoon activities, more marginal angles to the field's story. In one two-bedroom house, nicely done up with art on the walls, a couple lies together with the electric blanket still on. They have had sex and they are talking.

"What do you mean? Why do I have to work so hard to understand you? Are you actually a cryptic puzzle?"

Pause.

"That is for you to decide"

Pause.

"I might get up."

Pause.

"Not much of a day though."

Pause.

Another disruption to play. There's a dog on the field, a huntaway Alsatian cross, just so happy that Bradley is running, so pleased to see Bradley and to run with him. Ears flapping. Spit flying. It's not the Crockly Bradley, it's the other Bradley, the postie Bradley with the dog. The game stops, and Rick is taken off. His leash has come apart, that's the trouble. And no wonder—Brad had made it with the solid rubber bands laying round the floor of his car, discarded from bundles of letters. Brad works as a postie, and when he found he'd left the old leather lead at home, he'd improvised, linking the rubber bands together. Rick was convinced about being on a lead as they set out, and when he was tied up, but it only takes one weak link… Twang! And you are free.

One of the old blokes gets the key and goes and puts Rick back in Brad's car. Rick knows that he's in a small spot of trouble. The rules about when you can run with Bradley and when you can't have a few variables and it is hard to stop and contain your joy and sum up the guidelines. When Bradley is richly sweaty and running his heart out, he likes his dog to bound along beside and Rick lives to be that dog, bounding. It's great. Maybe, now, the trouble was the other young males running too, running tangled, a tangled pack. Warmer in the car, with the pleasing smell of Bradley, Rick settles down on Bradley's postal-uniform jumper, nose between paws, for a nap.

Natalie sharpens her pencil. She stands up to stretch briefly, takes her thermos out and pours half a beaker of tea, warms her hands before broaching a task that must be done to perfection: delineating the underside of the leaf. Straightening the stool and settling onto it again, she thinks herself back into the glowing green, soft translucence, hopeful fragility. She begins shading with fine soft lines.

The work takes time, but the drawing is exactly what she intended.

It's taken Natalie some time to move from drawing for the product, a fine sketch, to drawing for process, total absorption that frees her from anxiety–and then finding that at the end there is also the product…

* * *

The Work That Is Invisible in Audit Sheets

And how much work do we academics do that goes nowhere? Have you laboured at research writing that did not make publication, submitted the perfect succinctly persuasive funding application that failed to win the money, prepared stunning teaching material for courses that were discontinued, put time into helping colleagues who could do with a hand, and then more time, because you get involved in their problems? As the only person in your family with flexible hours, have you picked up caregiving chores during the day and then needed to make up the time on marking, class preparation, writing for deadlines in the evening while your family dozed in front of the tv?

Tempting metaphors for such work are "work in the shadows" or "work that slips down the cracks." There will be many times when you help people who do not repay that help; somehow, though, you make the environment more benign by helping. Sometimes the candidates you have given your time to will withdraw from their doctorate, having got a good job, or decided to spend their lives differently. Colleagues can pull out of projects that you are committed to, or be dismayingly tardy at making their contributions. Things can change. But much success, that work out in the sunshine and visible to all, achieves solidity because it is supported by the credit and accrued expertise built through work that can't be audited.

Am I being too positive here? Well, I think that is the way to go.

Caspar Henderson (2013) provides a model of optimism towards care that persuades me. In an extraordinary book that builds a personal philosophy of ecological responsibility into the shape of a medieval bestiary, Henderson makes the case that hopelessness is not an excuse for not marvelling and caring (Henderson, 2013, 94–96). A comment in the marginalia summarises the three laws of thermodynamics as: "(1) You can't win. (2) You can't even break even. (3) You can't get out of the game." Then Henderson has a paragraph from Bertrand Russell, including "The whole temple of Man's [*sic*] achievements must inevitably be buried beneath the debris of a universe in ruins… only on the firm foundation of unyielding despair can the soul's habitation be safely built." Steadily throughout a rich and beautiful book, Henderson goes on to celebrate the little "miracles of life."

That same desire to value what matters and sustain it even while aware of what is unravelling has been expressed of academia: a rally cry asking academics "to foster compassion for our mutually frail humanity" adds "express gratitude, hold out hope, be quick to find humour, cultivate indifference to convention and a willingness for insubordination" (Harré, Grant, Locke, & Sturm, 2017, p. 7). These aspirations are folded within vision of the university as a space where the "infinite game" of ongoing intellectual inquiry can play out. That is the kind of optimism that this book in your hands wants to inspire in you. You are right to approach the academic environment critically, and at times it is almost certain you will do so with justifiable despair. But this awareness of the darker reality is the firm foundation that frees you to celebrate yourself, and shape yourself. Despite logical awareness of futility amongst the ironies of the academic career, you can notice the miracles of learning, get to savour "the magical things patiently waiting for our wits to grow sharper" (Russell, cited in Henderson, 2013, p. 95) and give service towards making the university the place where you want to work, and actually, to spend your life.

The trick, then, once you have established who you want to be, and how you want your life to play out, is to learn how to build a story of that, a story that is coherent and persuasive. The genre of applications for promotion, funding and self-reporting requires control of rhetoric for the story of who you are and what you contribute.

Putting Service in Its Place: Developing from the Inside

I taught ACADPRAC 702: *Academic Citizenship and Professionalism* between 2016 and 2019. The course had been designed some ten years earlier within a postgraduate certificate, and then altered over successive iterations. "Students" were almost always early-career academics wanting support with their professional growth. More than that: they were academics who wanted to dig critically into what professionalism meant, and to shine at what they did. The course was predicated upon the way that "academic identity [is] constantly under reconstruction, emerging through and embodied in cumulative experiences of varied and complex intentions, actions and interactions with others" (Amundsen & McAlpine, 2011, p. 39). In an institution where many academic contracts spell out an expectation that time would be split into 40% for teaching, 40% for research, and 20% for service, "academic citizenship," half the title of the course, seemed a different turn of phrase for "service." Citizenship entails helping things to run, to run ethically. Just as citizens pay tax, academics pay their dues in their service. And "professionalism" seemed a curious social class term that we explored.

Not all those who undertake the Postgraduate Certificate in Academic Practice come from our institution, and many of those who do are on a relatively recent contract, the Professional Teaching Fellow (PTF) contract. PTF's career shapes are built around 80% teaching and 20% service. Their contracts don't include time for research. For many of these academics, the lack of research is a relief—they thrive on the exhilaration of prompting learning. For other new doctoral graduates, the PTF is the only contract on offer, and it means they will work double time to achieve the publication that might make them eligible for the job they really want, the traditional 40/40/20 lectureship. The certificate class in 2018 was a mixed cohort on a variety of contracts, with different aspirations. What follows is the pummelling we gave to the course's key terms with a battery of questions. I'm hoping that these questions will prompt you to reflect on your own answers to them in relation to your own academic environment.

Citizenship in its widest sense: is this about compliance with rules? Is it about rights? Is it about democracy? At what levels does citizenship need to be enacted: in-house, in your own neighbourhood, nationally, internationally? Then how might citizenship apply at different levels…? How does awareness of citizenship map onto personal identity and daily practice? Does citizenship have any connection to place and race? Is there any link to national identity? Patriotism? Conservativism? Commitment? King and country, state and people? Is this about following the leader? How *blindly* does the citizen follow to be an ideal citizen?

We dug about in the sociolinguistic slippage: is citizenship about kindness, empathy, ethics, morality, equity, loyalty, sociality, putting others first…? And might that term also stand for exclusivity, judgement, suspended critique, unquestioning compliancy..? Does this double-sided term tag along with vicious extremism about who is in and who is out, as well as with the kindness of strangers? There are theories on citizenship. Xiudi Zhang (2018, p. 63), who draws on multiple theories while reviewing ideas of citizenship, views "citizenship not only as the formal relationship between an individual and the state but also as between individual citizens and the local community or family where identity, institutional practices and a sense of belonging emerge from these social connections (Lister, 2016; Somers, 1993)." You could begin with these references that Zhang cites if you want to read more about the slithery nuances of responsibility and privilege wrapped together in the term "citizenship."

Academic citizenship raises the same set of issues and questions within an academic framework: it plays out at different levels, in classes, department/school, institutionally, internationally, extramurally… How might academics involve themselves in the positive aspect of citizenship within the different levels of their work? What is the connection to discipline and research teams? Is there any link to discipline identity? Does academic citizenship raise questions about what constitutes good leadership? Each of those in that 2018 classroom considered how awareness of citizenship mapped onto their personal identity and daily practice. Again, what work realities mix within citizenship: kindness, empathy, ethics, morality, equity, loyalty, sociality, putting others first? Does good academic citizenship entail prioritising and strategising, putting your own work first for contribution to research, saying no to requests for help; in its rigour, does it mean gatekeeping, exclusivity, judgement, and suspended critique of senior management decisions…? How do we manage ourselves as good academic citizens?

The perimeters of the word *professionalism* were checked, beginning with ideas of expertise, savvy, know-how, responsibility and trustworthiness. I asked "What does professionalism mean to you in your career? Could it mean something about true leadership?" Then we questioned whether professionalism was about playing the role, *acting the part* of academic/teacher/researcher, by wearing better clothes and speaking more guardedly and with better enunciation. Do we strive for that enunciation because it fosters inclusivity, making it more likely that international students will hear us, or to sound upmarket, like people who our parents were not? Does professionalism make you less "one of the people"? There is a pejorative, "a bloke in a suit": does *professional* really guarantee trustworthiness or might it imply the opposite, someone with authority whose decisions may harm? Amongst the talk, we found a real ambivalence between professionalism's guardedness when it means that nothing is openly stated, and the way that openness may reveal stupidity rather than truth-saying.

This chapter offers a mid-chapter exercise to invite you to personalise what academic citizenship and professionalism might mean in your neck of the woods. Firstly, identify the challenges of your academic environment. As I wrote this at the start of 2018, I perceive my challenges to be not the difficulty with journal acceptance, or student numbers—those issues seem more or less ubiquitous, and I am accustomed to them by now. I'm more angered by the times when my institution makes stupid choices that take us to the theatre of the absurd. Your grievances may well differ from mine. I suggest that you itemise what bugs you about academia, and about your own particular situation, your own institution, the realness of the habitus you work within.

Draw up two columns, with a bright side on the left and its shadow darkness on the right. Here's my list of challenges as an example:

Dichotomies, Paradox, Irony

Your list might not be of paradoxes, although my hunch is that it might be too. Listing them gives something to push against in shaping your own future. It's a reminder that when you know your own strengths and limitations, you will probably still have challenges you might bring yourself to address.

In ACADPRAC 702, the academic development safe haven provided a place to air dissatisfaction unguardedly, which surfaced the realisation that we shared the same feelings and were not alone. When we were done with that, the talk about the abstract nouns (citizenship, academic citizenship, professionalism) delineating an ideal academic self slid into something deeper. We'd begun thinking about how to be a better professional by developing better strategies that could be demonstrated with evidence when applying for promotion. But we moved along. We wanted something more inspiring than that. We looked into the possibility that, in a time of change, this is a ripe season for redefining ourselves as academics, licensing ourselves to choose how we will teach, research and give service.

We considered the extent to which we had the ability to choose direction based on desires, interests and personal values needs to be taken up. Ahmed picks up on the linguistic evocation of the term "desire lines" (Ahmed, 2006): "in landscape architecture they use the term 'desire lines' to describe unofficial paths, those marks left on the ground to show everyday comings and goings, where people deviate from the path they are meant to follow" (Ahmed, 2006, pp. 19–20). She stresses agency, the right to choose and the obligation to self to choose authentically. If academic career development is seen as the line followed, Ahmed's case applies: "to follow a line takes time, energy and resources, which means that the 'line' one takes does not stay apart from the line of one's life" (Ahmed, 2006, p. 17). The personal and the professional are inevitably interwoven.

Work/life balance ought not to be only about time management strategies to keep work contained. It should consider how a whole life approach can enfold external lives (families, love interests, sport, art, music, travel… the things that keep us human) to those we build within the institution. The career line we build within the institution should be designed to keep us human too. "If we give up on the line that we have given our time to, then we give up more than a line; we give up a certain life we have lived, which can feel like giving up on ourselves" (Ahmed, 2006, p. 18). Academic citizenship and professionalism, the service component of an academic contract, allow for individual desires to be enacted. There is scope there for the imagination to be the source of inspiration.

Terms like "inspiration" and "soul" evoke spirituality and yet their bothersome religious background ought not make this a no-go zone. The higher education environ that I am familiar with is secular. A secular environment means a more diverse one, which is pleasingly open and inclusive, but which sidesteps talk about education as the development of soul. As Sean Sturm and I put it,

> The word "soul" might sound off-puttingly non-secular for some; for us, it emphasizes education's connection to what is most authentic about us, whether conceived as subjective (our "inner self") or intersubjective (our "humanity"). Education… is about values, ethical and aesthetic (about what is good and beautiful) in action. (Sturm & Carter, 2015, p. 42)

I brought to ACADPRAC 702 my desire to surface core values so that those in the class could inspect their own meaning-making and consider the service aspect of their career in relation to anagogic calling. I carried the Sturm and Carter (2015) desire to "ensoul" career development even within neoliberal academia. In the first of six classes, I asked these academics to do a brief self-audit of personal values. I was worried that this might be too personal, too warm and fuzzy, yet in a class peopled by an astrophysicist, several engineers, and an architect, amongst others, the exercise went well. That led me to think maybe it is useful, and to want to write this book.

Logging up irony

Academic freedom	Strategic funding drying up research in arts and humanities
Inclusivity that looks like equity	Inclusivity that looks like exploitation of more and more young "clients" because it is based on a business growth model
Institutional rhetoric that sounds heartwarming	Decisions made by accountants that go against that rhetoric
Institutional desire for increased research impact via publication	Increasing demands that academics waste time with bureaucracy as professional staff are decimated to cut costs
Active advertising to attract more international doctoral students	Reduction in learning advisor support for them
Nicely developed democratic processes that factor in consultation	Power brokerage through something like a medieval court system, with decisions made behind closed doors by a few individuals, "consultation" a meaningless charade, and everyone knowing that you waste time spent in giving feedback on proposed changes
A holistic system for evaluating academic performance, e.g., for promotion	Decision-makers who nonetheless value publication over leadership in service and teaching

Challenges, then, should be (1) acknowledged; and (2) viewed in the context of your own individual particularity. We academics can celebrate that academia does offer a fair degree of intellectual freedom. We can purpose our imaginations to test that freedom, and perhaps to make the world ethically stronger in terms of values and aesthetics. Ahmed offers a constructive challenge, that we "…keep open the possibility of changing directions and of finding other paths, perhaps those that do not clear a common ground, where we can respond with joy to what goes astray" (Ahmed, 2006, p. 178). The trick is finding joy in the small aspects of our academic life where we can sometimes plot our direction according to our own desire lines.

The first text-box exercise below could be done individually; it also works well in seminars where people trust each other reasonably well. The second one aims to take what you are mulling over out to your academic community.

> Step up above your academic work and review it from the perspective of a cheerful cynic. What is ironic at your institution?
>
> What is ordinary about working in a university? Take a *workerly* approach to what you do.
>
> Take on the role of personal academic developer for yourself. Describe what is tough now. Then step in as professional to ask why does this really matter? Does it really matter? What do you learn about yourself that this bothers you? What steps can you take to find solutions? Who can you seek help from?
>
> What do you bring to your work in terms of street smarts, wisdom picked up from friends, from family or from life experience?
>
> What stories from your life's experience can be overlaid onto your academic work as extended metaphors?
>
> And what do you need to do in your life to sustain yourself when you get troubled? List a couple of pleasure providers you should draw on more often. Then follow your own advice.

> Try checking what your students do not know. You could use technology to allow anonymous response. What is the range of ignorance?
>
> Talk to colleagues about whether what bugs you also bugs them. Check what they think. You should either bond in recognising shared experience, or they may be able to direct you to help or solution.

References

Ahmed, S. (2006). *Queer phenomenology: Orientations, objects, others.* Durham, UK: Durham University Press.

Aitchison, C., Catterall, J., Ross, P. I., & Burgin, S. (2012). "Tough love and tears": Learning doctoral writing in the sciences. *Higher Education Research & Development, 31*(4), 435–447.

Aitchison, C., & Guerin, C. (2014). Writing groups, pedagogy, theory, practice: An introduction. In C. Aitchison & C. Guerin (Eds.), *Writing groups for doctoral education and beyond: Innovations in theory and practice* (pp. 3–17). London, UK: Routledge.

Aitchison, C., & Lee, A. (2006). Research writing: Problems and pedagogies. *Teaching in Higher Education, 11*(3), 265–278.

AkldUni4Schools. (2010). University of Auckland lecturer on unicycle with student on his shoulders – juggling!!!. Retrieved from https://www.youtube.com/watch?v=PuhhpBJtMTw

Amundsen, C., & McAlpine, L. (2011). New academics as supervisors: A steep learning curve with challenges, tensions and pleasures. In L. McAlpine & C. Amundsen (Eds.), *Doctoral education: Research-based strategies for doctoral students, supervisors and administrators* (pp. 37–55). Dordrecht, The Netherlands: Springer.

Becher, T., & Trowler, P. (2001). *Academic tribes and territories: Intellectual enquiry and the culture of disciplines* (2nd ed.). Philadelphia, PA: Open University Press.

Bell, M., & Cooper, P. (2013). Peer observation of teaching in university departments: A framework for implementation. *International Journal for Academic Development, 18*(1), 60–73.

Bernstein, D. J. (2008). Peer review and the evaluation of the intellectual work of teaching. *Change, 40*(2), 48–51.

Bill, A. (2017). Counter-conduct in creative university research: Deliberations on freedom. *Higher Education Research & Development, 36*(2), 241–254.

Bloom, B. S. (1965). *Taxonomy of educational objectives: The classification of educational goals.* New York, NY: David McKay.

Carruthers, M. J. (1990). *The book of memory: A study of memory in medieval culture.* Cambridge, UK: Cambridge University Press.

Carruthers, M. J., & Ziolkowski, J. M. (Eds.). (2002). *The medieval craft of memory: An anthology of texts and pictures.* Philadelphia, PA: University of Pennsylvania Press.

Carter, S. (2012). Original knowledge, gender and the word's mythology: Voicing the doctorate. *Arts and Humanities in Higher Education, 11*(4), 406–417.

Carter, S., Kensington-Miller, B., & Courtney, M. (2017a). Doctoral supervision practice: What's the problem and how can we help academics? *Journal of*

Perspectives in Applied Academic Practice, 5(1), 13–22. https://doi.org/10.14297/jpaap.v5i1.235
Cleveland-Innes, M., & Campbell, P. (2012). Emotional presence, learning, and the online learning environment. *The International Review of Research in Open and Distance Learning, 13*(4), 269–292.
Cosh, J. (1998). Peer observation: A reflective model. *ELT Journal, 53*(1), 22–27.
Garrett, G., & Davies, G. (2010). *Herding cats: Being advice to aspiring academic and research leaders.* Axminster, UK: Triarchy Press.
Garrison, D. R., Anderson, T., & Archer, W. (2000). Critical inquiry in a text-based environment: Computer conferencing in higher education. *The Internet and Higher Education, 2*(2–3), 87–105.
Harré, N., Grant, B. M., Locke, K., & Sturm, S. (2017). The university as an infinite game: Revitalising activism in the academy. *Australian Universities Review, 59*(2), 5–13.
Henderson, C. (2013). *The book of barely imagined beings: A 21st century bestiary.* Chicago, IL: University of Chicago.
Kamler, B., & Thomson, P. (2006). *Helping doctoral students write: Pedagogies for supervision.* London, UK: Routledge.
Kelly, F. (2015). A day in the life (and death) of a public university. *Higher Education Research Development, 34*(6), 1153–1163.
Kensington-Miller, B., & Carter, S. (2019). 'Permission to write': Building a community of inter-disciplinary writers. *Journal of Perspectives in Applied Academic Practice, 7*(1), 1–10.
King, S. (2000). *On writing: A memoir of the craft.* New York, NY: Scribener.
Lamott, A. (1995). *Bird by bird: Some instructions for writing and life.* New York, NY: Anchor.
Lister, R. (2016). Citizenship, welfare rights and local government. In J. Demaine & H. Entwistle (Eds.), *Beyond communitarianism: Citizenship, politics and education* (pp. 163–178). Basingstoke, UK: Palgrave Macmillan.
MacFarlane, B. (2007). *The academic citizen: The virtue of service in university life.* London, UK: Routledge.
Marton, F., & Saljo, R. (1976). On qualitative differences in learning: Outcome and process. *British Journal of Educational Psychology, 46*, 4–11.
Meyer, J. H. F., & Land, R. (2005). Threshold concepts and troublesome knowledge (2): Epistemological considerations and a conceptual framework for teaching and learning. *Higher Education, 39*, 373–388.
Negus, K., & Pickering, M. (2004). *Creativity, communication and cultural value.* London, UK: Sage.
Pelias, R. J. (2004). *A methodology of the heart: Evoking academic and daily life.* New York, NY: AltaMira Press.
Shea, P., & Bidjerano, T. (2009). Community of inquiry as a theoretical framework to foster "epistemic engagement" and "cognitive presence" in online education. *Computers & Education, 52*(3), 543–553.

Siddiqui, Z. S., Jonas-Dwyer, D., & Carr, S. E. (2007). Twelve tips for peer observation of teaching. *Medical Teacher, 29*, 297–800.

Silvia, P. (2010). *How to write a lot: A practical guide to productive academic writing* (6th ed.). Washington, DC: APA Life Tools.

Somers, M. R. (1993). Citizenship and the place of the public sphere: Law, community, and political culture in the transition to democracy. *American Sociological Review, 58*(5), 587–620.

Sparkes, A. C. (2007). Embodiment, academics and the audit culture: A story seeking consideration. *Qualitative Research, 7*(4), 521–550.

Sturm, S., & Carter, S. (2015). From Eden to Agora: The e-learning trading zone. *Critical Studies in Teaching and Learning (CriSTaL), 3*(2), 40–59. https://doi.org/10.14426/cristal.v3i2.48

Sword, H. (2017). *Air and light and time and space.* Cambridge, MA: Harvard University Press.

Thesen, L. (2014). "If they're not laughing, watch out!": Emotion and risk in postgraduate writing groups. In C. Aitcheson & C. Guerin (Eds.), *Writing groups for the doctorate and beyond: Innovations in practice and theory* (pp. 172–176). London, UK: Routledge.

Watkins, D., & Biggs, J. B. (1996). *The Chinese learner: Cultural, psychological and contextual influences.* Hong Kong/Melbourne, VIC: University of Hong Kong Comparative Education Research Centre; Australian Council for Educational Research.

Zhang, X. (2017). *Flying kites: How Chinese international students in New Zealand reflect on Chinese citizenship.* (Doctoral thesis). University of Auckland, Auckland, New Zealand.

CHAPTER 5

Taking Stock of Identity During Change

Abstract This chapter directly confronts the instability of academic employment that is more common in the current neoliberal environment and considers how academics can best cope with changes that may be forced upon them. It draws upon borderland crossing theory, and on inspiration from medieval literature's constructions of heroism and leadership as those aspirations might be applied to academic endurance. This is a chapter about recognising what survives, able to be adapted. It suggests how professional identity and integrity might be held intact when subjected to institutional change managers at work. The story in this chapter pays tribute to longitudinality, to death and to what we carry with us that we inherit from those who have gone before us.

Keywords Academic borderland crossing • Stories as identity markers • "Leadership" • Cross-disciplinarity • Self-audit exercise

Academic Borderland Crossing: Tough Terrain, Stories as Coinage for Identity

I'm making a bid for optimism and determination within the current academic environment where employment conditions are arguably trickier to negotiate than they were in the twentieth century. You are likely to be aware of "the reformation of the very nature of education in instrumental terms connected to business and the economy: the transformation of

S. Carter, *Academic Identity and the Place of Stories*,
https://doi.org/10.1007/978-3-030-43601-8_5

students into 'consumers'; and the degradation of pay and working conditions for academics, as well as the increasing casualisation of employment" (Gill, 2009, p. 230). A fairly large Australian study found descriptors from casualised academics "palpable: *miserable*, *embittered*, *shattered*, *suffering*, *isolated*, *worn out*, *swamped*, *stressed* and *dissatisfied*" (Bosanquet et al., 2016). Debowski (2012, p. 194) points out that "careers are likely to take many turns and … your preparation for serendipitous chance events, multiple career paths, and maximizing your talents will be critical" (citing Raabe et al., 2007). A new academic career grows harder to establish (see Austin, 2002; Cantwell, 2011; Wheaton, 2020). Academics pull their identities together with "a sense of constantly being judged in different ways, by different means, according to different criteria, through different agents and agencies… [and] being constantly accountable, and constantly recorded" (Ball, 2003, p. 220). Kidman, Chu, Fernandez, and Abella (2015) offer a specific example with Māori, who may have conquered a socio-economic glass ceiling, but who nonetheless have more trouble than those who came into academia a generation ahead of them. "These days Māori academics more often identify with a middle class, and yet have less sense of job security than the generation of Māori scholars before them" (Kidman et al., 2015, p. 10). Archer observes that "the impact of new managerialism and performativity… has been to render all academic identities more unstable" (Archer, 2008, p. 401). To survive within a massified and internationalised tertiary education system, we must learn how to adopt new ways of being (Cantwell & Scevak, 2010; Debowski, 2012). Enforced shapeshifting can be demoralising, but, as Harris (2006, p. 430) suggests, academics need "to resist deterministic and pessimistic analyses of current problems" when caught up in transition that is sometimes necessary. Instead, and against a great weight of rage and disappointment, they need "to recognize the possibilities and opportunities" in the current volatile climate (S. Harris, 2006, p. 421). Frequently, the discomfort of change is felt more pressingly than its opportunities. Sureness of your own core identity, self-knowledge and self-confidence are needed at such times. It is worth recognising the crux of who you are through the self-reflection this book aims to prompt. Knowing the value of who you are gives you the best chance of strength and flexibility for times of pressure and times of change.

The next section considers how to handle the arid deserts of academia that sometimes need to be crossed in order to find better spaces for work that you actually enjoy doing. Gloria Anzaldua's (1987) theorising of the border crossing makes a model for using the discomfort of borderlands to establish your own values, resistance, and definition. During transitions, you need self-sustenance. Can you draw a narrative thread from values you inherit from your family, and the skills that you have picked up along the way, to show that, even when restructuring engulfs you, you should be celebrating yourself within your work? Itemising familiar methods, ideas, and artefacts that prove adaptable in a new work situation can be helpful. The lessons from one environment, the values built from that learning, provide some kind of stability for other performances. Taking stock in a reflective narrative makes meanings of experience; such reflective storying "resonate[s], grow[s] and sustain[s] identities" (Churchman & King, 2009, p. 515). Survival stories about transitions of one sort or another are helpful in establishing that this is what we do. Listening to stories and figuring out what these stories mean give a route to not only understanding what happens but changing what happens by understanding it. Frances Kelly has produced a book interrogating the doctorate through fiction that included characters who are doctoral candidates and supervisors (Kelly, 2017). Kelly is a higher educationalist and erstwhile literary scholar who analyses the ideas found in fiction to show how they reveal social beliefs. Kelly speculates that:

> Perhaps we tell old stories and tall stories, familiar and well-worn stories, troubling and uncanny stories and ideas about the PhD to counter the current discourse that highlights the bland utility and usefulness of the PhD for national and global knowledge economies. (p. 12)

Her approach and observation acknowledge the power of stories, in this case as push-backs against neoliberalism. Kelly's book is well worth reading if the processes of the doctorate interest you—the literature she covers sounds really interesting. The book is worth reading too, for its method of crossing between the genres of educational investigation and literary analysis (the sort of work that I did when I described Passmore doing on the Loathly Lady tale). By insisting that there is trade between fiction and experience, Kelly allows for readings both ways, and that seems to me how imaginations work. Imaginations make connections. In doing that, they make meanings evident.

Amongst sense-making from stories, and discipline expertise, and the stories that we construct ourselves about our experience, we build ourselves. As an example of reflection that sustains during transition, I'm going to describe my shift from teaching medieval and early modern literature to a higher education placement constructing, developing and coordinating a cross-discipline doctoral programme.

My career shift seemed sensible, because in New Zealand there was not a great deal of work teaching medieval literature when I graduated from the University of Toronto and returned home to be closer to aging parents. My move into the uneasy identity of learning advisor/academic developer (Alexander, 2005; Chanock, East, & Maxwell, 2004, pp. 43–52) began with teaching and counselling people who I admire: doctoral students. I was charged with developing a coherent, generic doctoral programme across disciplines. I'd learned critical reading skills in literature studies, and saw my research opening in doctoral education as close-reading the "text" of the doctorate's social exchanges (Carter, 2014). Teaching was rewarding: doctoral students welcomed advice on managing supervisors, sussing what a PhD was, understanding what examiners needed to see, showing critical analysis in their writing, and learning how to contextualise their own research within a broader discourse. Academic development provides a cross-disciplinary vantage point from which to observe and investigate the tensions and disjunctions of the doctorate. I wanted to research what I was seeing. To publish, I had to fit into a different discourse community, those talking about higher education rather than about medieval literature.

A Shapeshifting Story

My borderland crossing set out from English medieval literature studies where I had learned to read earlier societies' values through the colour, violence, and irony of their literature. From immersion in early legends, I took away insights that persist in how I view the world. The warrior ethos of patient endurance in those early stories had a masculinist flavour, and yet seemed pertinent to twenty-first-century female challenges. The following rally cry seems applicable to handling crises in life relating to care-giving and aging, and yet this is not the feel-good modern age speaking: this epithet has the sharp-edged valour of a Battle of Maldon warrior about to be hacked to death in 991:

> Purpose shall be the firmer, heart the keener, courage shall be the more, as our might lessens… (Donaldson, 1993, p. 75)

That resolve suggests a screen-shot of the valiant hero handsomely dripping battle gore, but it adapts well for caregiving, too, for accompanying the long, hesitant shuffles down the passage to the toilet, and the slow hours spent hanging in through the relentless frustration of decline. My literature studies feed into my life, something I can draw upon as an academic under pressure. We do not die with our backs to the wall within the role of academic precariat (Ruccio, 2017), but perhaps we do need to actively rally ourselves towards taking control when the situation shifts during enforced change.

A jargon term supplied currently in the application for promotion forms at the institution I work in is "leadership." Each section asks "How do you demonstrate leadership in teaching, research, service…" Old stories are all about leadership. And, yes, we do all demonstrate it as we broach a heavy wave of marking, or labour in unfamiliar software to change how we teach a class. "Leadership is all about getting results. You stand or fall by your ability to 'get the job done'" (Garrett & Davies, 2010, p. 21). That work ethic accords with many family values as well as being embedded in stories of heroism.

I'm aware, then, that my higher education identity is built on the values underlying medieval literature and theory. The literature is often quirky, full of ironies and inversions—maybe because of this, it gives legends still helpful in twenty-first-century academia, which is also a place of ironies. Medieval literature studies gave a strong grounding to understanding teaching and learning. In the same way that multiple takes on medieval artefacts enable a richer interpretation of them (Martin, 1992), so do multiple takes on teaching and learning enrich understanding. Medievalists have fascination with the elusive, the quest for the sublime, or at least, what is noumenal rather than phenomenal. Often yarns made vivid by lust and violence were underpinned by a religious concern for soul. Soul—or core identity—was always the real issue.

The search for what matters inheres in medieval study. Artefacts, including old stories, are often just fragments, and scholars then puzzle to make sense of them. Figuring out the concerns of past societies can lead to the truths their stories teach about the present. For example, Caroline Walker Bynum compares medieval obsession with the body/soul dualism to relatively recent fictions showing that human anxiety and fascination with it continue in fictions such as *The Brain* and *Max Headroom* (Bynum, 1991, p. 247). Carolyn Dinshaw (1999, p. 184) launches a Foucauldian comparison between medieval and postmodern treatment of raised-and-repressed homosexuality from the title "Getting medieval." That's a sadistic punch-line from the Tarantino film ***Pulp Fiction***: "Hear me talkin', hillbilly boy? I ain't through with you by a damn sight. I'm gonna get medieval on your ass." She shows how the film follows narrative twists comparable to those in *Sir Gawain and the Green Knight* (circa late fourteenth century). Nothing much changes. Difference is often only apparent: deeper levels of thinking remain, sometimes worryingly.

Connections across centuries, such as those Bynum and Dinshaw make, begin from strange medieval interests that seem obviously odd; by showing how similar these are to what we still trouble ourselves with, they defamiliarise the modern, opening up our own familiar culture for critique. When the familiar is defamiliarised, self-knowledge becomes unavoidable. We approach contemporary culture with fresh eyes. Both the unfamiliarity and the familiarity of the medieval world make it an excellent entry point to English literature studies (Carter & Poole, 2012), the field of my doctorate. The next step was to apply that same approach of defamiliarisation to the study of education. The learning advisor overview meant that I was not comfortably embedded within an epistemological framework, and the shared acceptance this provides within discourse communities (Laurs & Carter, 2013). Working across disciplines allows access to strategies, methods and theories from many. It also allows cross-disciplinary questioning of how these work. Trade across borders, leveraging off both difference and similarity, was familiar to me from medieval studies. Becoming a learning advisor in some ways felt more promising than staying enfolded in the small, esoteric field I had made my own as a PhD student.

It should be acknowledged that learning advisors are a troubled species by all accounts. They suffer from the lack of a discipline (Mitchell, 2006). They can feel that they are regarded as second-class, for example, when they are referred to as "the writing lady" by discipline-centred academics (Alexander, 2005). Kate Chanock notes that we are regarded as doing "remedial" work, often relieving students' literary constipation, responding to "it's all in there—I just can't get it out" (Chanock, 1995, p. 33). Catherine Manathunga (2007) applies Homi Bhabha's cultural displacement theory and suggests that learning advisors are academic "refugees" (Manathunga, 2007). But in a season when academia recoils from neoliberal assaults, learning advisors work strategically for causes that matter: opening the door so that students can cross those learning thresholds (see

Phipps, 2013). Target groups are often those who have been historically marginalised (Van Rij-Heyligers, 2005): cultural groups who are under-represented in graduation figures, first-generation students, older students and any who feel alienated within academia. Arguably, amongst the usual frustrations and challenges of academia (Austin, 2002; McNair, 1997; Morley, 2003), the learning advisors' central mandate is especially rewarding: to enable access to success more broadly. Working specifically with doctoral students from across campus took me into terrain that is exhilarating and sometimes frightening. Yet the generic vantage point is now my entry point to research. Now as an academic developer I am in a familiar trading zone, brokering across borderlands, happily handling shifts in shape.

Billot (2010, p. 713), seeking to reconcile managerialist and traditional academic values, notes the importance of "a fluid identity" or "the development of transitory identities"; borderlands theory draws on the ambivalence of transition, the potential for benefit and need for survival strategies when inhabiting such identities (Laurs & Carter, 2012). Winter (2009) finds a schism between values that are congruent and incongruent with managerial discourse, resulting in a "fractured work environment" where higher education identity becomes "lost" (2009, p. 121). He suggests that academics have "inner" and "outer" professional identities (p. 122), a split caused by guardedness in the face of new managerialism as they either align with or "separate themselves from the demands of a corporate enterprise" (p. 123). Academics engaged in "narrative identity development" (McLean & Pasupathi, 2012, p. 13) tell stories that counter those expansionist success tales identified by Churchman and King (2009, p. 508) as proliferating in institutional rhetoric. Yet borderland crossing theory notes that transitions are more nuanced than this, belying a clear dualism of either alignment with, or separation from, managerialism. I suggest here that, like a self-audit of values, reflection on transition can affirm confidence and engagement with the current academic environment.

An Example of Self-Audit

You could itemise what you take with you into different teaching and research areas. I took the pleasures of studying medieval literature, and its potential to draw out insights into social values and obsessions into my teaching as a learning advisor and academic developer.

- First, social values were visible in the medieval rhetoric under the close-reading scrutiny; many of us in higher education peel back the rhetoric of our institutions to unearth the subtext's values, which give us leverage for action.
- Second, medieval values are seen at enough of a distance to be laughable—Monty Python's *Holy Grail*, for example, capitalised on the ridiculousness of some medieval stories; academics will be happier if they retain a sense of humour towards irony in the current environment.
- Third, the social values of the medieval text are to be found to be still internalised within society and within the academy, raising questions about whether we want that or not. Medieval text is often sexist when the ideal woman is lovely and cup-bearing, and the ideal male, the strongest and smartest in the land. Then there's blind loyalty to social superiors fuelling a willingness to charge in questionable directions—in the twenty-first century, we might want to reconsider.
- Most importantly, teaching and learning, and the development of a researcher identity, are affective processes that allow for growth at anagogic levels. The ensoulment of teaching and learning is still what matters.

Painful transition sometimes prompts learning at its richest. Often, distancing and defamiliarising make higher education practice more visible—which is useful for both teaching and research. Honing values, with an acceptance of instability, makes it more possible to find a personal identity within a contested zone. Each of us finds our path through the social dimensions of academia (see Brookfield, 2006; Bruffee, 1999). We should aim to be amongst the more comfortable hybrids, "the Academic Chameleon and the Resolute Researcher" (Barry, Berg, & Chandler, 2006, p. 275), from a set of academic identities that includes "the Stressed Professor." Phillips and Hardy speak of "the power of incomplete, ambiguous and contradictory discourses to produce a social reality that we experience as real and solid" (Phillips & Hardy, 2002, pp. 1–2); such fractured discourses speak individuals into being. Articulating what holds firm constructs a sense of continuity and refinement, rather than loss and abandonment from workplace shifts due to downsizing or restructuring.

I speculate that this particular form of reflective practice will inevitably grow more important as we head further into a century distinguished for the "adaptability" or uberisation required from its workers. While Billot

(2010, p. 717) argues that "there is a need to align institutional and personal objectives" and that such a mission should not overlook the multidimensionality of personal objectives as academia flexes under change. I'm not promoting a situation of frequent change as ideal, but suggesting that academics need strategies of coping with adaptation to remain fulfilled and functional in each new environment. The Loathly Lady's early Irish hero Niall was rewarded for accepting what was "many-shaped" and somehow energetically engaging. A self-audit of the approaches, attitudes and skills that remain intact is the heuristic model on offer here. I'm finishing this section on transitions with another short story about the bigger picture that enfolds academic objectives.

* * *

The Bigger Picture: Longitudinal Influences

Time present and time past
Are both perhaps present in time future,
And time future contained in time past.
If all time is eternally present
All time is redeemable.
—T. S. Eliot, *Burnt Norton*, first of *Four Quartets* (1968)

I woke to a beautiful morning, a pink tinge visible through the slats of the balcony. The air outside was soft, scented with datura flowers. He had wanted fine weather for his funeral. Well, he was getting his own way there.

This death feels like a direct hit, but I'm not making a fuss. I hate women weeping. I hate their snot, their malleability, their viscous self-indulgence. I hate the feel-good inanity of "it's ok to cry." Frankly, I'd rather you didn't.

I never like being left behind. This death brought on a new feeling, a threshold feeling.

Marion came on time, exactly. Her car was iridescent green like an exotic beetle's wings and almost brand new. Driving there, the little car purred along through the motorway lanes and turned off to the early autumn landscape of green angular hills, the plains cut by lines of bare trees, and, later, the forested hills leaning down to the winding road.

Conversation along the way was careful. Our children, how sensible and successful they were. And how nice they were. The setbacks, cautiously, along with truisms about the bright side of life. How lucky we have been. We didn't remember the times inhabited by our younger and less wise selves. I regret that I once threw a pretty bone-china teacup in the direction of her head so that it smashed on the wall behind her.

We parked well down the road and walked to the house. The black workshop truck was decorated out with ponga fronds, a good keen bloke's sort of hearse. The coffin set on the porch was decked with hibiscus flowers. A large tarpaulin defined the funeral space outside on the front lawn. Chairs in convenient rows were probably from the local hall. Photos on several pin boards set up against the porch railings showed how sunny this life had been. Grinning at the helm with huge seas mounting behind him. A young man, jaunty, in a stylish leather waistcoat. I knew the woman who made the waistcoat so cleverly, so stylishly. I knew the story of who it had been for, and why they didn't get it, who bought it, and how it was given to become part of this man's persona. The man with his golden-haired son, and Anna, his golden-haired wife, smiling. The smiles in these pictures show real exuberance. Love, and joy.

"Why had this good man died when there were so many crappy people still alive out there?" asked Anna.

This was a boy who grew up biking across the fens to the sea with his sister: her letter from England told the story of his childhood and adolescence, the stage of his life when he dropped out, listened to Joan Baez and Bob Dylan, moved to the city. This was a man who danced, for hours and with everyone, at the parties he organised. This was a deep-sea sailor who summed up the situation accurately, did what needed doing, and could handle the storms. The best father you could have had for the golden-haired boy. A man who did only what he wanted to do but it was always the right thing to do. And all the rest of us wanted to do it too, or to be there as part of what he was doing. This man was a quiet leader. He was generous with time, energy, enthusiasm. These were the people; this, the man.

Stories were told, refuted—"no, we didn't get the wood from a shed, it was out the back under a macrocarpa, and we had to carry it up a hill, it was bloody hard work"—and reframed, with verdicts cast from people who might have been at the edges, as to which was the right story, whose car it was, where the truck had broken down, who suggested it first. Stories were constructed in teams, with bit characters from them chipping in: "I was one of those kids and I definitely remember that the deal was: if we could wake him up, we got a ride to school on the back of the truck on his way to the workshop. There were usually about a dozen of us. It wouldn't be allowed today." The old tearoom legends were paraded again: "A man who is mean with jam is mean with life," with retorts about people who hog all the jam. Collectively assembling our memories around this man we found we had come together as a body, the richer for being made up of odd bits and pieces. Our stories just touched the sides.

I can't leave the long, steady path uphill to the cemetery that the teenage boys struggled up with the coffin, stopping once to put it down for a breather.

And I'm not able to keep my feet within the genre of short-story-telling involving funerals, a genre lively with denouement. Lovers or business partners emerge from the woodwork; people learn ludicrous truths about the dead beloved. Read Alan Bennett, *The Laying on of Hands: A Story*. There's a story for you. Short-story funerals are richer than Christmas for bringing out the worst in people, their meanest natures regarding their nearest and dearest, and the unwelcome truths, once hidden, that nestle amongst professionally constructed wreaths. The death of the body in a fictional funeral activates a satisfying cerebral cynicism. Everyone is shabby and small in the light of death. Funeral stories are often beautifully crafted; how a true short-story writer must savour shaking off the hormonal, stepping up to the limitations of flesh and cuttingly critiquing love through death.

But here I find, too far through to turn back, that Johnny's funeral doesn't yield material for such a short story. This is about a real death, a well-crafted death—he died beautifully cared for at home—and its realness is holding me back from crafting his funeral's story. The failed lovers and business partners were all there, pleased to be with each other, sheepish perhaps, but more comfortable for being older. I can't step aside from the earthly facts of the matter: I am grateful for that man, the golden-haired woman still alive and lovely, this life, that day, those people, this body of friends, especially the ones at my side. I cannot bring myself to craft this anymore obligingly. In Aotearoa New Zealand it is a commonplace to say that we each carry our dead with us.

I learned the right term for the verb tense "present perfect" only when, scrounging around for work between my limited-term academic contracts, I taught English as a second language: the present perfect is the tense English uses when what has happened in the past continues to affect the present. An example is "Our friend has died." There aren't endings, except sometimes in fiction. Life isn't like that. The present is rendered perfect by the effects of the past. We carry the dead along with us and must act out their energy.

Two text-box exercises follow. The first is individual, and there's actually two suggestions that both aim to help you contextualise yourself longitudinally. The second is a group exercise hoping that collaborative cognition might be productive working from prompts to thinking outside the box… just a bit outside the box.

Think about times of change or challenge in your academic career to date. Tell the story of what shifted, why it shifted and what you have carried with you nonetheless from one domain to another. Remember what was hard, what was interesting and new, and what or who sustained you through the change. What stays the same through change?

Then consider someone who influenced your trajectory, who they were, what qualities you admire and want to emulate.

A game around imagined possibilities, courtesy of the word "if"…

Here's some conversation prompts for group work with academics. First everyone has a few minutes to think and make notes, and then there's discussion.

The prompts

A. If you were to win a HUGE amount of money, what changes to your life would you make immediately?
B. If you were employed as a change manager at your tertiary institution, what changes would you consider making? Any that you would make immediately?
C. If you were starting tertiary education again as a first-year student, what courses would you take—would you widen your area of expertise?

The goal of this conversation is to prompt consideration of what matters to you (A); what you consider most important to academia (B); and whether there are ways that you might ideally re-position yourself, perhaps in collaboration or perhaps just slightly, by reading in different discourse strands (C).

References

Alexander, K. (2005). Liminal identities and institutional positioning: On becoming a "writing lady" in the academy. *Inkshed, 22*(3), 5–16.

Anzaldua, G. (1987). *Borderlands/La Frontera: The new Mestiza*. San Francisco, CA: Aunt Lute Books.

Archer, L. (2008). Younger academics' constructions of "authenticity", "success" and professional identity. *Studies in Higher Education, 33*(4), 385–403.

Austin, A. E. (2002). Creating a bridge to the future: Preparing new faculty to face changing expectations in a shifting context. *The Review of Higher Education, 26*(2), 119–144.

Ball, S. J. (2003). The teacher's soul and the terrors of performativity. *Journal of Education Policy, 18*(2), 215–228.

Barry, J., Berg, E., & Chandler, J. (2006). Academic shape-shifting: Gender, management and identities in Sweden and England. *Organization, 13*(2), 275–308.

Billot, J. (2010). The imagined and the real: The tensions for academic identity. *Higher Education and Research Development, 29*(6), 709–721.

Bosanquet, A., Mailey, A., Matthews, K. E., & Lodge, J. M. (2016). Redefining 'early career in academia: A collective narrative approach. *Higher Education and Research Development, 36*(5), 890–902.

Brookfield, S. D. (2006). *The skillfull teacher: On technique, trust, and responsiveness in the classroom* (2nd ed.). San Francisco, CA: Jossey-Bass.

Bruffee, K. A. (1999). *Collaborative learning: Higher education, interdependence, and the authority of knowledge* (2nd ed.). Baltimore, MD: The Johns Hopkins Press.

Bynum, C. W. (1991). *Fragmentation and redemption: Essays on gender and the human body in medieval religion*. New York, NY: Zone Books.

Cantwell, R. (2011). Academic in-sourcing: International postdoctoral employment and new modes of academic production. *Journal of Higher Education Policy and Management, 33*(2), 102–114.

Cantwell, R., & Scevak, J. (2010). *An academic life: A handbook for new academics*. Camberwell, UK: ACER.

Carter, S. (2012). Original knowledge, gender and the word's mythology: Voicing the doctorate. *Arts and Humanities in Higher Education, 11*(4), 406–417.

Carter, S. (2014). The methodology of magpies. *International Journal of Research & Method in Education, 37*(2), 125–136.

Carter, S., & Poole, R. (2012). Threshold to discipline discourse: An English literature first year course. *Australian Journal of Language and Literacy, 35*(1), 69–81.

Chanock, K. (1995). Counselling and academic skills teaching: What person-centred counselling can tell us about person-centred skills teaching. In M. Garner, K. Chanock, & R. Clerehan (Eds.), *Academic skills advising:*

Towards a discipline (pp. 29–37). Melbourne, VIC: Victorian Language and Learning Network.
Chanock, K., East, J., & Maxwell, J. (2004). Academic and/or general? How the classification of LAS advisors affects us and our institutions. *Language and Academic Skills in Higher Education, 6*, 37–45.
Churchman, D., & King, S. (2009). Academic practice in transition: Hidden stories of academic identities. *Teaching in Higher Education, 14*(5), 507–516.
Debowski, S. (2012). *The new academic: A strategic handbook.* New York, NY: Open University Press.
Dinshaw, C. (1999). *Getting medieval: Sexualities and communities, pre- and post-modern.* Durham, NC: Duke University Press.
Donaldson, E. T. (1993). The Battle of Maldon. In M. H. Abrams (Ed.), *The Norton anthology: English literature* (Vol. 1, pp. 70–75). New York, NY: W. W. Norton and Co..
Garrett, G., & Davies, G. (2010). *Herding cats: Being advice to aspiring academic and research leaders.* Axminster, UK: Triarchy Press.
Gill, R. (2009). Breaking the silence: The hidden injuries of neo-liberal academia. In R. Flood & R. Gill (Eds.), *Secrecy and silence in the research process: Feminist reflections* (pp. 228–244). London, UK: Routledge.
Harris, S. (2006). Rethinking academic identities in neo-liberal times. *Teaching in Higher Education, 10*(4), 421–433.
Kelly, F. (2017). *The idea of the PhD: The doctorate in the twenty-first century.* London, UK: Routledge.
Kidman, F., Chu, C., Fernandez, S., & Abella, I. (2015). *Māori scholars and the university.* Wellington, NZ: Victoria University of Wellington.
Laurs, D., & Carter, S. (2013, November). *Learning advisors and doctoral border-crossing: Negotiating those frontiers.* Paper presented at the Annual International Conference of the Association of Tertiary Learning Advisors of Aotearoa/New Zealand, Christchurch.
Manathunga, C. (2007). "Unhomely" academic developer identities: More post-colonial explorations. *International Journal for Academic Development, 12*(1), 25–34.
Martin, P. (1992). Chaucer and feminism: A magpie view. In J. Dor (Ed.), *"A wyf ther was": Essays in honour of Paule Mertens-Frock* (pp. 235–246). Liege, Belgium: University of Liege Press.
McLean, K. C., & Pasupathi, M. (2012). Process of identity: Where I am and how I got there. *An International Journal of Theory and Research, 12*(1), 8–28.
McNair, S. (1997). Is there a crisis? Does it matter? In R. Barnett & A. Griffin (Eds.), *The end of knowledge in higher education* (pp. 27–38). London, UK: Cassell.
Mitchell, C. (2006, November). *A + B = 1:1, formula required? Reflections on learning development and one-to-one teaching from a new learning development*

tutor. Paper presented at the Anchoring our practice: Perspectives, partnerships, projections, Tauranga.
Morley, L. (2003). *Quality and power in higher education.* Philadelphia, PA: Society for Research into Higher Education & Open University Press.
Phillips, N., & Hardy, C. (2002). *Discourse analysis: Investigating processes of social construction.* London, UK: Sage.
Phipps, A. (2013). Intercultural ethics: Questions of methods in language and intercultural communication. *Language and Intercultural Communication, 13*(1), 10–26.
Raabe B, Frese, M., & Beehr, T. A. (2007). Action regulation theory and career self-management. *Journal of Vocational Behavior, 70*(2): 297–311.
Ruccio, D. F. (2017). Academic precariat. Retrieved from https://rwer.wordpress.com/2017/04/16/academic-precariat/
Van Rij-Heyligers, J. A. (2005). *Globalisation and pluri-scalar orchestrations in higher education: Locating the University of Auckland's Student Learning Centre historically and globally.* University of Auckland, NZ: EdD.
Wheaton, A. (2020). Shift happens: Moving from the ivory tower to the mushroom factory. *Higher Education Research & Development, 39*(1), 67–80.
Winter, R. (2009). Academic manager or managed academic?: Academic identity schisms in Higher Education. *Journal of Higher Education Policy and Management, 31*(2), 121–131.

CHAPTER 6

Personalising Professionalism: Balance, Risk, Chance, Change…

Abstract This chapter returns to the theme of a holistic mesh between life and academic career, insisting that personal values and preferences make good foundations for academic development. It includes a short exemplar from Andrew Withy, philosophy lecturer, on what motivates him as an academic. Imaginative intelligence is considered along with the potential of extended metaphors for reaching new understanding. The chapter includes some strategies for life that I have drawn from chess, sailing and literature studies to suggest that lessons from life make up some of academic identity. The story is about going to a dance in an unfamiliar city.

Keywords Work-life balance • Personal motivation • Fate • Metacognition • Lessons from life • Parable

Academic careers are built in and out of life, with its own lively communities, our friends and our families. It is commonplace to talk about "work/life balance," often by sharing tips for being better organised, and making sure that you do take annual leave. I propose that we might share the impulse to push back against neoliberal bureaucracy, and deliberately seek alternative focus for political and personal pleasure. Paul Sutton (2014, p. 4) regrets, in a confessional rallying call, that this takes conscious effort:

S. Carter, *Academic Identity and the Place of Stories*,
https://doi.org/10.1007/978-3-030-43601-8_6

> Often, in the numerous meetings I attend, I have compromised my academic integrity as a progressive educator by a fatalistic conformity to bureaucratic directives, by a resigned acceptance of yet more performativity. Often, I have colluded in the mass production of students through delivering standardized models… Often, I have simply accepted the fatefulness of neoliberalism and managerialism.

Sutton (2014, p. 4) cites Freire (1998, p. 102) for recognition that such a fatalism allows "the bureaucratization of the mind". Separating work and life overlooks the inherent connections between them in individual lives, which are lived holistically. Drawing life and work together enables a healthy holism. Every aspect of life makes us who we are. Relationships with friends and family members sometimes need to override work chores, and work relationships are often, and perhaps should be, as meaningful as extramural ones. José Luis Gonzalés-Geraldo once said firmly, "We are people before we are professionals," in a private conversation from about six years ago, during which I explained that Edie's illness might mean I didn't join him to give our paper at a conference. His sentence has formed another of the legends relating to academic development in my schemata: being a person allows us to be just a person, with human limitations. There's no shame in that. And then we also have the responsibility of human capacity for inspiration, creativity and aspiration.

Andrew Withy compounded my sense that in universities we need to privilege people, and additionally, that it's worthwhile articulating what energises our academic careers and helps us to persist. In a short ACADPRAC 702 exercise, where the class were asked to write about what most motivates their academic work, Withy wrote:

> What gets me up each morning is how my students learn. I like to see and hear their growth, observe how their understanding subtly changes, and watch as they explore and discover new things. I may not teach better than those around me, but I teach people, rather than content. I try to influence and assist people in ways that impact their lives. It's not that I like students individually or en masse (though some are fine); it's more that I like them as their eyes light up, and they can do things that they couldn't before. I'm a learning/understanding junkie, and want to spread the habit. There's a vicarious thrill to watching people discover for the first time things that have become old friends to me. I get to do this, not because I'm good with reading or caring about people, but because my priority as a PTF [Professional Teaching Fellow] is teaching, rather than research. I can put my emotional

> & intellectual energy into the course, submerging myself and my students more deeply. I can live the course along with them, and thus be a genuine companion on their journey. I have also been a student until recently, so can relate to some of their experiences more readily.

Withy's reflection captures the exhilaration available amongst the pressure of academia. Managing life and career is a balancing exercise. Friendship and family give ideal models for making academic relationships more meaningful, and then the real intensity of academic pleasure comes from sharing obsessions with others. Like Withy, Eva Bendix Petersen also drew on drug addiction as an analogy for academic addiction, in her case, addiction for our topics rather than for teaching. As a guest speaker at a conference, she gestured across a crowded lecture theatre and declared that, while we saw ourselves busy academics, she saw a roomful of junkies, waiting for the next hit of research time, and delighted when students show a love for our field because then we can peddle our expertise to them and share the pleasure of partaking (Petersen, 2012). That analogy is a dark one, and yet its positive offering is the recognition that academia gives something truly real, really vivid, vividly significant amongst life's experiences.

The interchange between life as an academic and as a human being beyond that coalesces in the imagination. Dreams will include work motifs—I'm late for a class, and they are sitting along the edge of a river, and there's a party going on—and friends and places from the past. I guess I'm struggling in this book to express the idea that we should defend our holistic selves and draw on that wholeness where it resides: in the imagination, that labyrinth made of memories taken from sensate experience and reflection upon these. Go back to the core to find our particular original contributions to academia: ourselves.

Handling Academic Changes: Finding a Stance for Endurance

Amongst the dark pleasure of obsessive addiction with learning's epiphanies and research's new knowledge, serendipity plays a considerable part in career development. Yielding to the fact that much of academic success depends on fate, fortune or chance allows for diminished anxiety. We can only do what needs doing boldly and as well as we can. As the warrior epic hero Beowulf puts it, "Fate goes ever as fate must"—that is Seamus

Heaney's (Heaney, 2000, p. 31) translation. The original was probably written around the millennium 1000 AD. Heaney translates one of my favourite lines from *Beowulf* as "fate often preserves the undoomed when his courage holds" (Heaney, 2000, p. 39). A more literal translation would be "Yet often, for undaunted courage, fate spares the man it has not already marked as doomed" (working from Jack, 1994, p. 62). Beowulf has a string of adventures that entail extraordinary perseverance and self-confidence. He recounts an unbelievable sea contest with a friend that entailed fighting off sea monsters in turbulent waters for three days. Later, because the cannibalistic monster Grendel haunting a mead hall is resistant to iron, Beowulf faces him bare-handed, overcoming Grendel by ripping off his arm. In this era, the mark of a hero was brute strength, while, as a nice touch to the story, Grendel's mum comes down for revenge and is a trickier, even more monstrous other to deal with—she's enraged, aggrieved and she's smarter. But it is the fire-belching dragon at the end who overpowers the then aging Beowulf as he kills it. That the story now sounds clichéd is because of the derivatives bred from it: *Beowulf* is the original. The story bred a genre, fantasy. Despite that Beowulf didn't attend to sustainability by breeding or training up a replacement for himself, that was one great leader.

Some academics seem to encounter the vicissitudes of academia more than I have, so their grapples with them are harder. I know several academics who surrendered important parts of their lives to further careers. They left their partners, their children, back home, to get a doctorate from a western university. They conducted their marriages across international borders so they could work where they might get tenure. I guess humans are like that: people risk their lives to earn livings. Academia does not overtly tell the stories of heroism when it means lengthy struggle managing emotions as well as workload. Most struggle stories stay hidden. They are told at home, as personal stories, only to most trusted confidants. Publically, we celebrate success, often with acclaim that exacerbates the chagrin of others whose funding or promotion applications were not successful. I feel that those who persist and fail deserve celebration, because theirs are stories about a more human kind of heroism: patience, endurance, and acceptance of slow methods to achieve a purpose. We need to celebrate courage itself rather than the success.

Imaginative Intelligence?

"Work/life balance" might be best managed by the imagination, with its reasoning and creativity. R. A. Finke and Bettle (1996) point out that there are organised thinkers and then there are chaotic thinkers—they developed an argument about best practice together after they noticed as collaborators that one of them was ordered and the other chaotic. They make a defence for chaotic cognition on the premise that "modern society has become excessively ordered and structured" (R. A. Finke & Bettle, 1996, p. vii), while suggesting that it is sensible to try to think differently from your natural inclination: if you are more comfortable planning and ordering, you should try to be more impulsive, and vice versa.

Thus far into this exercise you will have thought quite a bit, I hope, about yourself and all the myriad experiences that construct your own particular imagination. What fruity mixture does your own fruitcake imaginary hold? We each have anecdotes that we recount probably too often, the stories about events that shaped us by frightening, or surprising, or amusing us. Acknowledging big chunky general frameworks like culture, gender, sexual preference only begins to describe the potentialities of our imaginations. Something like a map of a large region might show rivers and major cities but leave out much that is significant to the reality of the region, the corner store, the empty sections, the trees, dogs and wobbly fences.

As academics, we might try to better understand ourselves in order to gain full benefit from the resources that we possess in our persons. My hunch is that we may be able to work by making use of both the overview map and the tiny details available when we zoom in, so that we can consider both the small delicacies of our practice and the big picture, the trees *and* the forest. As academics, can we deliberately work from metacognitive overview to the sensate reality of experience? John Flavell (1979, p. 906) describes metacognitive knowledge as "stored world knowledge that has to do with people as cognitive creatures" and points to its potential. It "can lead you to select, evaluate, revise and abandon cognitive task, goals and strategies in light of their relationship with one another and with your own abilities and interests..." (p. 908). This is relevant to the academic career: we are commonly obliged to prioritise what gets done first and what languishes on the back-burner—where often it is writing projects that are left congealing and unattended. It may be possible, as we select our goals, to do so with attention to our individual preferences, values and desires, bringing imagination into play a little more deliberately as we zoom in on the particulars of our terrain.

Willingness to step sideways and to see our work freshly sometimes shows up new possibilities too. Mark Johnson (1987, pp. 127–137) carefully elaborates how medical break-throughs in the first half of the twentieth century were enabled by a shift in metaphorical frame from the body as machine to the body as homeostatic organism. (I'm doing something similar by moving discussion of work/life balance from a set of tips for improved strategies in different aspects of work to an approach that meshes work and life together as one symbiotic system and works with the chaos of that.) When the body was regarded as a machine, treatment involved repairing and replacing parts; later, the parts were viewed as part of the whole, and treatment shifted to maintaining and restoring "the body's functional balances" (p. 130). Johnson explains the steps that led Hans Selye to challenge the perspective of his medical training by offering the fact that wellness and disease are not a dichotomy but exist on a spectrum. Selye noticed that once you are unwell with almost anything, you begin to exhibit symptoms of stress and that these stressers undermine health. As Johnson puts it, "disease is a matter of degree" (1987, p. 135). Maybe we could deliberately try changing metaphors when we get to impasses in research work or in our career development to see whether that lets us slither sideways into new understanding.

Johnson's (1987) point with the example, though, is not to offer a sure-fire route to intellectual break-throughs, but rather to suggest that sometimes our understanding is constrained by the schemata that shape our disciplines. His "enriched view of understanding" is based upon

> ...one's way of being in, or having, a world. This is very much a matter of one's embodiment, that is, of perceptual mechanisms, patterns of discrimination, motor programs, and various bodily skills. And it is equally a matter of our embeddedness within culture, language, institutions, and historical traditions... It might be more satisfactory to say that our understanding is our bodily, cultural, linguistic, historical situatedness in, and towards our, world. (Johnson, 1987, pp. 137–138)

The view so neatly frames up an exercise of self-audit as the foundation of academic career development. Punter (2007, p. 68) echoes Johnson's argument, noting that "subjectivity is not formed in isolation, but rather in cultural, social and political contexts." And Punter goes further, deciding that it is "the continuous activity of metaphorising that makes us human..." (Punter, 2007, p. 56). He points out that "life in itself is intrinsically metaphorical" (p. 105). This seems to nudge towards the idea of viewing the challenges of academia not with despair or depression, but at least as a puzzle, if not actually a game involving metaphoric resonance and depth, ideally, the "infinite game" (Harré et al., 2017).

Life experience can be read metaphorically for metacognitive insight, too. I have three examples to demonstrate what I mean. The first was one I learned as a novice sailor. Left at the tiller, I was initially always nervous about whether pulling it towards me or pushing it away would encourage the 32-foot *Terral* to lift her prow towards the direction I needed. It took three waves rolling through before it was clear which way I had turned her. I learned to trust myself for three waves' space of time before deciding whether I had got it right, or whether I needed to haul the boat back the other way. Knowing to stay patient and wait before deciding whether a choice was the wrong one is applicable to an academic career. Often in academia we must perform visibly at tasks we have never done before, where there is little or no guidance and a delay before the outcome is clear. For example, curriculum change usually intends better alignment of learning outcomes and careers, while students' and/or colleagues' may show a marked lack of enthusiasm for such change. It may be worth a couple of iterations of the changed curriculum to see whether attitudes turn to the positive, and the course lifts back on a sure course.

The second example of a lesson from life was learning to play chess, and having it explained to me that the chess queen was the most powerful and therefore most valuable piece. She is strong, regal and strategically capable. As a novice player, I dreaded using her in case I lost her because I wasn't savvy enough to see her grief coming. Only after losing the game a few times without using the queen did I know I prefer to lose the game with my queen lost than to lose the game with my queen unused. The lesson for life that taught me was to focus on the game rather than on accounting for all the pieces, and to willingly risk my best piece. Each piece should be used as purposely as possible. Each has a role to play.

Art, with its resonant signalling, often offers metaphors for living. Literary scholarship unpicks meaning, and in that process, may find messages dense with advice. Edmund Spenser, writing in the late sixteenth century, had perhaps pondered on the risk of losing his best warrior-heroine, too. In his poetic investigation of morality and political endeavour, he directs Britomart with writing above the door about a life-or-death decision she must make:

> And as she lookt about, she did behold,
> How ouer that same dore was likewise writ,
> *Be bold, be bold*, and euery where *Be bold...*

Yet a few lines later Britomart is cautioned "*Be not too bold...*" (*The Faerie Queene*, Book III; Canto Vi, Stanza 54, in Hamilton, 1997, p. 412). The distinction between being bold and not too bold seems relevant to being an academic. Because I studied *The Faerie Queene* and taught it, it sits in my imagination amongst other frameworks. You will most likely have your own scholarship impinging on your sense-making imagination. Consider for a moment whether that is the case and, if it is, consider the way that scholarship contributes to the schemata that enable you to make meaning of life. Life experiences include educational ones.

Each of us differs along some strung-out Likert scale of aversion to risk and our willingness to trust ourselves. What is certain is that there is no sure way to know when to risk one's most valuable assets and how to evaluate accurately when to be bold and when bold might turn into too bold.

The accumulation of such experiences and lessons for life makes for individual value. Rather than tending to notice limitations, it is possible to audit and respect those values. Virginia King describes how to make a metaphorical map of self as researcher and academic and provides her own map, noting "gaps at the centre of my island, where one might imagine a sickle-shaped mountain range [that] represents the academic qualifications I lack" (V. King, 2003, p. 99). This is an exercise she facilitates with colleagues and students. How would you draw a map of self in a landscape that is metaphorical? Which bits might be swampy? Where are your tourist hot-spots? I'm seeking the questions to ask you, and to ask myself, that might carry us forward into something more rewarding, a better understanding of ourselves and how to get the most from those selves. Take on the role of geographer and describe yourself as territory. Then, as a geographer, consider the allies, enemies, trader-partners and colonies that sustain your kingdom. Become the advisor who recommends possible actions for sustainability and improvement.

Stepping into the Grizzly Rose Country Bar, Nightclub and Music Hall

Now, if you were travelling on research leave through Denver and found out there was an enormous saloon with live country and western music and a big dance floor putting on a show that very night, would you be tempted? Country and western in the USA... The evocative name of the Grizzly Rose saloon did it for me. We set off into the night.

The bus left the residential lines of homes and headed into an unlit industrial zone that was punctuated by the bright colour of an occasional liquor store. We hopped off at our stop by one of these, and followed our walking instructions in light drizzle. The well-lit through-road fell away behind us. The side road took us into a spread of large factory buildings, heading towards a distant, buzzing motorway at the end of the road. It didn't look right.

Just when our optimism was wavering towards turning back, there it was, the longed for neon flash of the Grizzly Rose. The door was hard to find, dark and looking locked. But it yielded, and we were in to pay our entry fee through a grill to a saloon-bar blonde. We sat at a table with our beers and watched the dancers.

This was a dancing community with its own quite particular rules. The bar stool cowboys here were dressed for the part, and most of the women wore cowboy boots. They were of mixed ages, with a preponderance of ours: old. And they took to the floor in pairs that varied. Some were really good at what was a mix of waltzing, foxtrot and three step. They were suave, poised, tall, slender, dressed in the gear with the fringes and tassels and perfectly partnered for a slick performance. Others were hopeless; they stumped round together with an occasional attempt at a twirl. One guy was really ancient and bent double—he just hobbled along while a woman patiently held onto him to prevent him from falling or being bumped over. Some were stiff and had L for learner written large in body language. But they were all happy, and they all showed the human capacity for the love of engagement and for pleasure. It was a joy to see them step around the floor.

Not so fast: there were traffic rules here. The entire body of dancers moved in a slow anti-clockwise spin. If partners twirled within their own orbits, they also orbited other partners. Think of water vortexing down the plughole. Was this our scene? I was dubious. Neale's enthusiasm took us onto the floor. I got over feeling self-conscious because different. We are all different.

The bus home was a long time coming, and passing cars thinned out, but we stood in the light drizzle knowing that, awkwardly and energetically, we'd shared in a dance that felt like a metaphor for being human. In a dance about being human.

The first text-box exercise is another that hopes to encourage self-knowledge, and more than that, self-recognition and self-development. The second exercise is a fairly pragmatic task that it is helpful to perform in a seminar with other academics whose insights can be shared.

So, another set of questions:

- Can you think of one time when you were nudged out of a conceptual framework during your non-academic life and then learned something from that? Summarise that, as see whether you can use it as a metaphor when you are teaching.
- Do you feel personally that you might prefer to lose having spent all your assets, or are you still saving them because you cannot bear loss? And do you wait out the waves that pattern your own life's oceans before reassessing your work? How much do you explore alone? How much do you take advice from others?
- What self do you construct by the assumptions that you take for granted? Is this your best possible self? Could you rewrite the legends writ above the door? Might you skew your metaphorical framework to see what happens? Should you listen more carefully to advice from others, even those you normally discount?

Revise your teaching philosophy, or write one if you haven't done so yet. Can you avoid clichés?

References

Finke, R. A., & Bettle, J. (1996). *Chaotic cognition: Principles and applications.* Mahwah, NJ: Lawrence Erlbaum Associates.

Flavell, J. H. (1979). Metacognition and cognitive monitoring: A new area of cognitive-developmental Inquiry. *American Psychologist, 34*(10), 906–911.

Freire, P. (1998). *Pedagogy of freedom: Ethics, democracy, and civic courage*. Oxford, UK: Rowman & Littlefield.

Hamilton, A. C. (Ed.). (1997). *The Spenser encyclopedia*. Toronto, ONT: University of Toronto Press.

Harré, N., Grant, B. M., Locke, K., & Sturm, S. (2017). The university as an infinite game: Revitalising activism in the academy. *Australian Universities Review, 59*(2), 5–13.

Heaney, S. (2000). *Beowulf*. New York, NY: Farrar, Straus & Giroux.

Jack, G. (Ed.). (1994). *Beowulf: A student edition*. Oxford, UK: Clarendon.

Johnson, M. (1987). *The body in the mind: The bodily basis of meaning, imagination and reason*. Chicago, IL: University of Chicago Press.

King, V. (2003). Self-portrait with mortar board: A study of academic identity using the map, the novel and the grid. *Higher Education Research & Development, 32*(1), 96–108.

Petersen, E. B. (2012, June). *Monsters astray in the flesh: A layered exploration of the im/possibilities of resistance-work in the neoliberalised university*. Paper presented at the Academic Identities Conference, University of Auckland.

Punter, D. (2007). *Metaphors*. London, UK: Routledge.

Sutton, P. (2014). A paradoxical academic identity: Fate, utopia and hope. *Teaching in Higher Education, 20*(1), 37–47. https://doi.org/10.1080/13562517.2014.957265

CHAPTER 7

Your Dance, Your Self, Your Story: The Fruitcake Imaginary

Abstract This chapter draws the books themes together and provides the climax to the book. It returns to the issue of imagination's relationship with body, metaphor and meaning-making, taking Mark Johnson's observation of imagination as the basis of reason further into imagination's creativity. Imagination and reflection are brought together. There's a tally of nine points that the book has made, with these points woven together throughout and now reaching culmination. They accumulate to a homily on a fruitcake, something homely and rich, designed to be shared, all of which is true of academic identity. The provision of recipe performs emphasis on homeliness, heritage and community. The story is a dream with a weird futurity—make of it what you will.

Keywords Imagination • Reason • Metaphor • Creativity • Fruitcake • Homily

Often we academics do not consciously think about academic self-construction; we simply scurry around daunting lists of chores that grow in resistance to our efforts to reduce them. At the same time, being an academic always involves hard learning. Every year, we are likely to undertake something for the first time, and often the consequences of our actions seem significant. We want to get things right. The academic career so often *can* be compared to stories of valiance. We create ourselves as we

S. Carter, *Academic Identity and the Place of Stories*,
https://doi.org/10.1007/978-3-030-43601-8_7

career through whatever challenges eventuate in our chapter of the epic, the "infinite game" of the university, where the purpose is not to win but to keep the game in play and bring in more players (Harré et al., 2017). The infinite game calls the imagination into play. Like the fruitcake imaginary, the infinite game is an enabling metaphor, allowing a new framework for considering the academic career.

Employing the Imagination

So, this book emphasises that an academic career within the context of the neoliberal third mission provides scope for the imagination. Mark Johnson is a trail-blazer in recognising the relationship of body and mind for the construction of thought, and in championing the way that metaphors can be extended into new dimensions of understanding. His argument about the imagination draws heavily on his own thoughts about metaphor (Lakoff & Johnson, 2003). Seeking a "complete theory of imagination" (p. 171), Johnson runs through his argument linkages: metaphoric types provide schemata that allow scaffolding for new ideas, scaffolding that he calls "metaphoric projections." He points out that "narrative structure" is how we make sense of the world, with its sensations, the metaphors bodily experience generates, the metaphoric projections of these that allow understanding of complexity.

Yet Johnson (1987) quite firmly distances himself from the creative side of imagination, and I strongly believe that recognising and factoring in creativity adds something valuable. Johnson notes that commonly "the term 'imagination' connotes artistic creativity, fantasy, scientific discovery, invention and novelty" (p. 139), linking this to the Romantic period, which doesn't interest him. He argues reason would not be possible without imagination; his focus is on reason. He is not interested in the way imagination opens up aspirational dimensions, the quest for the sublime, enabled by creative and lateral thinking. Thus he holds back from the full potential of imagination. Yet, in noticing that reason and imagination are linked, the poet Shelley, writing in 1821 (Abrams, 1993), preempts Johnson, and willingly goes further, into the potential of art to sustain the spirit. Whereas Johnson sees imagination as crucial to enable reason, with reason as most important, Shelley turns that round, to see imagination as more important, and reason as supporting it.

> Reason is the enumeration of quantities already known; imagination is the perception of the value of those quantities, both separately and as a whole. Reason respects the differences, and imagination the similitudes of things. Reason is to the imagination as the instrument to the agent, as the body to the spirit, as the shadow to the substance. (Shelley, in Abrams (Ed.), 1993, p. 753)

I began the book wanting to suggest that factoring in imagination's more creative functionality allows us to be ourselves more fully, more productively, and more satisfyingly. I'm finishing by feeling surer that such development makes the university a better place all round. "The great instrument of moral good is the imagination," wrote Shelley (Abrams, 1993, p. 759)—he was writing to champion art as more important than ever in what was seen (and celebrated) as the age of science and instrumentalism. There's a parallel in the current academic environment where imagination can push back against the idea that the university is first and foremost a business. Such a push-back equates with an academic quest for moral good.

I'm arguing that making use of cultural artefacts provides an ethical—moral and aesthetical—approach to a neoliberalism. Punter acclaims the humanising potential of metaphor and hence imagination, showing how literary tropes ripple out a wide range of social and political commentary (Punter, 2007). Academics have the capacity to use their imaginations beyond the building of positivist worlds; we can draw on the artistic and anagogic functionality of imagination. For example, bringing a wise clown into a historical fiction means questioning power hierarchies and privileging the cathartic power of humour and the ambiguities of individual identities. I suspect that it is not just good learning outcomes, curricula and digital affordances that bring magic into teaching and learning, but awareness of cultural artefacts available for employment in the interest of teaching and learning. For example, academic developers may find that adopting the wise-clown persona in seminars helpfully opens up discussion around institutional managerialism.

Most of us want to effect change within the academic environment. To what extent is it possible to get leverage for practice by privileging the individual imagination? As Negus and Pickering (2004, p. 9) insist, "Imagination remains key to thinking about creativity because it is continually regarded as the source of challenge to rules and conventions, as a way of recombining different aspects of tradition and knowledge…and perhaps most importantly, as a means to move beyond existing horizons of experience." It is not usually possible to turn back those big tides that are mainly instigated by a managerial focus on money. It probably helps to laugh rather than rage at the dark ironies of academic neoliberalism. Importantly, though, it is almost always possible to change small things, and to make universities places where kindness is still to be found. Earlier, I drew upon Johnson's (1987) observation that it is only our imagination that allows us to make sense of the world, to inhabit and to *have* a world. Adding together reflection on what we want academia to be like, and who we are as possessors of imaginations, and what values we want to champion, and what strengths we have to do so gives a form of academic development. The visual *mise en abyme* makes a symbol of the work that imagination and reflection can do together in the development of academic identity.

I am grateful to Evija Trofimova for her comment after reviewing an earlier draft of this book: she pointed out that imagination sometimes occurs spontaneously, whereas I'm recommending something that is deliberately summoned for a premeditated purpose. Evija gave "a child imagining a world of wonder" as an example of a free and spontaneous use of imagination. Now, my memory of my childhood's "over-active imagination" leads me to speculate that back then it provided an antidote to boredom. That is me, the adult, analysing what that past child was up to—I was not consciously scheming how to relieve the monotony of a rather dull (safe and sustaining, but dull) childhood at the time. As adults, though, we usually draw on metacognitive skills to get traction. Maybe using the playful or the anagogic potential of the imagination is something that as adults we might learn to manage, like we manage time, projects, self, emotions…

In line with the genre conventions for conclusions, here's a tally of the points made in this book towards academic identity development.

1. Theory can be used to defend creativity, and to allow you take things further.
2. Most probably your entry point to academia was the doctorate, an initiation, the liminal transition where academic identity is constructed—that experience means you have experience of change.
3. Stories convey meaning, and your own stories can teach you a considerable amount that is of use to your academic development.

4. Your street wisdom helps too; all those moments of sensate experience that have accumulated to give you a unique imagination, the capacity to make meaning of your life.
5. You can draw on metaphorisation as a method enabling complex thought, and then go further with extended metaphors, parable, exegesis and hermeneutic meaning-making, actively interpreting what you find around you.
6. Examples from groups strongly inflected by culture model how to draw upon culture as a tap-root.
7. Artefacts from culture, including popular culture, may be inspiring, and can be used to give soul to teaching, research and service.
8. The time-honoured elitism of academia may be an attraction for you at some basic level, but don't let it throw you off sureness in your own inherent knowledge; do you give your own background, culture, individual strengths and quirks enough recognition?
9. Academic identity is shaped by actions and relational performance. You have the stage and the entitlement to make something of yourself here.

Alongside academic responsibilities jostle life responsibilities so that academic identity accommodates multiple roles that need to be woven together into something coherent and comfortable. Academic developers and learning advisors have meta-expertise in development; this book invites you to develop that metacognition about your own development and take responsibility for your own well-being and development.

Teaching, research and service skill-sets should each be developed with consideration for your own body, experiences, imaginative landscape, preferences and values. Theories on learning are helpful for self-reporting but need critique through your own teaching experience; you should trust what you see, and respond to it. Deep reflection on your teaching experience should help with plotting skill development; then theory allows you to turn common sense into something scholarly. Authors who write about writing process can be inspiring for research writing, something you need to take seriously if you are expected to publish. The compulsion to give service is an invitation for you to fulfil your own potential as a community elder. You may be young, I hasten to add, but as an academic you hold community responsibility.

Fruitcake Ruminations

I began this book by explaining its beginning, the wet bush around colleagues from the Centre for Learning and Research in Higher Education, all of us working together on writing. When asked in that warm collegial setting what I was working on, I'd joked that this would be "one fruitcake of a book." That was to defuse how risky the project felt with its self-exposure, and its desire to pull together ideas about academic self-maintenance. But the inclusion of the fruitcake motif has become more than a joke. The fruitcake imaginary is something like an extended metaphor and this section runs with "making a fruitcake" as homily on "making an academic identity." A fruitcake recipe makes a metaphor for the argument that the book makes: that who you are results from myriad life experiences that construct your imagination. Who you are is a rich combination, like a fruitcake. You should share that self-abundance, as you would share a fruitcake.

To both ground and extend the imaginary, I'm concluding with the family recipe for a dark, rich fruitcake. In a small notebook, which was once mum's, the fruitcake recipe page in my handwriting is patina-ed by egg and butter, showing something stained by life as well as useful: well-used. To work between theory and practice, I reiterate that family heritage, stained and useful, adds foundational values and patterns to the construction of imagination.

Life; Work; Balance

The recipe for a fruitcake comes from my sister's husband's family, but has been used in my family for decades, mostly at Christmas. My sister is dead now, and I think of her and her story when I make this cake. My sister's demise was slow, and our afternoons together with me at work made it sustainable for me to spend more time with her (over about a decade) than a demanding full-time job usually allows. Karen Pittman (2005, p. 148) captures a similar experience movingly: "'I'm just going to grade these papers, Ma.' These were the last words I ever spoke aloud to my Mother." That so resonates with the hours I spent working in a companionable room with my sister as her health worsened: I wrote or marked, able to stop to put on the kettle, or to produce small treats to share, or to listen when she wanted to talk. Academia is demanding, and yet it also gives privileges not all workers have; many other intelligent workers have work rosters that are non-negotiable, so that when you need wages to live on, you just cannot spend time in caregiving. I don't recommend a lack of criticality towards the twenty-first century university, but I do recommend that old-fashioned extortion to count your blessings. No, let's be qualitative rather than quantitative in framing. It is not the *counting* that matters, but the seeing and savouring, and finding meaning in. This book asks you, dear reader, to try out a possible new academic genre that stretches towards kitchen-smell homeliness: look for every chance of pleasure in your whole life, where academic performance doesn't compete with, or conflict with, your extramural self. Making a slow-cooking cake that will please family and friends, you can be writing your next article, filling in a grant application, or tackling the grading (Fig. 7.1).

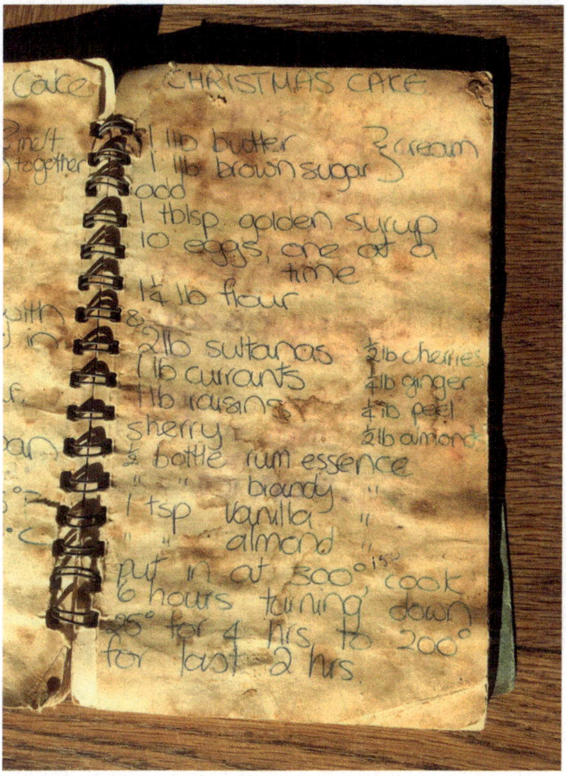

Fig. 7.1 Mum's recipe notebook that I still use: do stains pass as evidence of impact on practice in a research audit culture? (Photo by author)

In the same way that doctoral students often begin with a list of literature to be read, you could prepare to make the cake by adding the ingredients to your shopping list:

1 lb. butter
1 lb. brown sugar
10 eggs
Golden syrup
1.25 lb. of flour
2 lb. sultanas
1 lb. currants
1 lb. raisins
0.5 lb. candied cherries
0.25 lb. crystalised ginger
0.25 lb. candied orange peel

Rum, brandy, vanilla and almond essences

The Fruitcake Imaginary

The list of cake ingredients for your shopping list parallels the idea that the book is something of a list of ingredients, the ingredients that build into a case about constructing an academic identity in the twenty-first century. So what have the book's ingredients been?

- The art and artifice of stories teach at multiple levels.
- We can use that fact about how stories work to re-story ourselves into a stronger reality.
- Games give an extended metaphor for academia, with the infinite game (Harré et al., 2017) giving a promising co-constructive model.
- In valuing imagination, we might draw on the philosophy of the grasshopper who chose playing.
- Idiosyncrasies build good foundations for "best possible self" identities.

Making this fruitcake imaginary is physically challenging: it is a big mix to wind into being. The short version of the methods runs as follows:

- Draw on what is strong in your family; push against what you reject from the safe space of love.
- Learn empathy.
- You have to laugh, including at yourself.

Then stepping back from the fruitcake as an imaginary, into the recipe that is captured here as a tribute to family and homeliness, you may decide to make a different cake—typing out the ingredients showed a lot of sugar, butter and eggs, and many prefer to avoid recipes like this, even if the amounts in each small piece are not heart-stopping. Maybe you need to use a recipe from your own grandmother, or your friends who share, or from the web, where everything exists. Here's our family's.

Fruitcake Praxis

Begin by buttering a large cake tin, 10 x 10 inches or equivalent, and lining it with buttery paper carefully pushed against the side of the tin so that the cake will be easy to decant. Turn the oven on to 300F (or 150C) degrees.

Cream together:
1 lb butter
1 lb brown sugar
Add 1 tablespoon golden syrup
10 eggs, one at a time
1/2 bottle rum essence (or a tablespoon of rum)
1/2 bottle brandy essence (or a tablespoon of brandy)
1 teaspoon vanilla essence
1 teaspoon almond essence
1.25 lb flour
Add the fruit and stir through
2 lb sultanas
1 lb currants
1 lb raisins
.5 lb candied cherries
.25 lb crystalised ginger
.25 lb candied orange peel

When the mixture seems to be even, pour, scoop and scrape it into the tin, ensuring that the surface of the mixture is smooth. Put it into the oven.

For the first four hours, turn the oven down 25 degrees every hour so that the cake is on 200 degrees for the final two hours. The entire cooking process takes six hours, but the final temperature is so low that should you forget the cake and go off to bed, it is likely to be still delicious, especially if you wake up, smell it, and leap into the kitchen to take it out of the oven sometime in the early morning. It's an expensive recipe, a generous cake, and one that is kindly towards forgetfulness.

Community of practice theory could be drawn up to lend mock gravitas to the inclusion of this recipe. It is good luck to be given a small slice from others' fruit cakes at Christmas, and to give yours away too—see network theory (e.g., Downes, 2012): fruitcake belongs at the nodes.

While this fruitcake cooks, list some of the potentialities you might develop over the next year, and then start work, with half your mind on that cake, and your responsibility with the stove dial. I'm hoping that reassurance from the warmth and comfort of a fruitcake cooking might sustain you while you consider reconstruction within the instability of the current academic climate. Am I really expecting you, the reader, to make this cake? Then share the cake with those within your circle of practice? That is such a nice and yet absurd idea.

It is always bothersome finishing academic publication on an upturn. It seems naïve, counter to critical theory. You will have figured all the backstories here that contain darkness, yet the book seeks an upturn, even while wanting to distance itself from the feel-good genre. Let's finish instead with something of a puzzle, a story that came from a curious dream that I had some years back and wrote down as a story. Finishing from the dream world gives the last word to imagination, endorsing the book's central argument that as academics we should value the accumulation of past experiences, cultural and individual values, and the shabby failures that teach us to be stronger and more compassionate. It endorses the use of story as a valid method of building an argument. Thomas and Reinertsen (2019, pp. 196—197) speculate "If we can write and theorise differently and acknowledge the dream works in our writing we hopefully challenge the dualisms, the binaries, the taken-for-granted….We open the opportunities to live well with uncertainties". They finish their book by "Speaking against giving up. / Speaking for courage. / Speaking for uncertainty. / Speaking for power. / Speaking for hope" (p. 199). It's a strong ending, I think. And to wind back to metaphor as meaning-making, and imagination as the engine of metaphor, I want to draw on David Punter's reminder that "the dream can never be read literally, for its very substance is a metaphor; but thus one might also claim that the point of a dream, if there is such a thing, is to 're-mind' the subject that without metaphor, the world would have no 'sense'" (Punter, 2007, p. 81). If dream is some kind of metaphor, this dream leaves the conclusion open ended, over to you to make the future what you will.

* * *

The Girl Who Fell in Love with a Salmon

Cat had been a volunteer now for three weeks. Her Care and Recuperation Advisor had suggested it as part of her recovery after the accident. Helping others worse off could help the convalescent to regain confidence. It was important not to get too inward. Cat was placed with Bruce, a Royal Society for the Protection of Literal Transformation Species (RSPLTS) officer. Bruce's work involved driving from the Western RSPLTS centre to keep track of the transformed human animals, assist them to learn to adapt, and keep records. He could get ethics committee approval to treat his records as scientific data, write it up, add to understanding, but usually he was happy enough just doing the caregiving role of ranger. The master's was as far as he wanted to go.

The arrangement was that he would collect her in the van. She didn't need to face going in to town in her condition. When the van pulled in to the driveway on the first day she hurried out and got in before the driver could undo his seat-belt. She wanted to begin without any awkwardness or formality. Then they headed off west to the hills. Bruce glanced at her but he didn't stare.

He had explained to her as they drove along, "When people transform because metaphors turn literal, it creates all kinds of problems. We've known for a long time that once humans are transformed into animals they are surprisingly bad at surviving in the wild.

"Well, there was Actaeon of course as a classical model. Tragic, there. The boy just panicked. They blamed Diana but they liked to attribute natural phenomena to the gods back then. Or goddesses, more precisely. Circe, too, with her herd of swine, was one of the very famous cases of literalisation. They didn't understand it back then, and we still don't really. But at least now we have policies and we do something to help them through the transition period.

"Some of the early Celtic cases weren't quite so bad. Early Irish seemed to take it in their stride. Étaín, for example, managed to retain her marital appeal as a scarlet fly. That takes some gumption. There was something about the Celts; they were willing to accept the unexpected. They made a go of it."

Within a few days Cat knew she liked Bruce. He mainly seemed to take her for granted. She felt comfortable in the van and pleased she had been allotted to the RSPLTS. The animals were interesting because you could see that they were really people. Bruce called them the LTs. You got out in the fresh air. At first Cat just helped in the mornings so that she didn't get too tired. But for the last week she had done the afternoon rounds too.

Bruce was pleased with how quickly Cat caught on. When she first began to break the rules by feeding the LTs, he looked grateful. "Our regulations are research based, of course, that's crucial, but it is still tough when you see them floundering around and they can't make a go of it. You wouldn't believe how hard it is for some of them."

"For a species that is meant to be logical, humans are really very hopeless at adapting."

"I understand that they have to be taught how to fend for themselves in the natural habitat. That is, the natural habitat of their new form. But it takes them ages. The simplest things. They are worse than baby animals. They have to unlearn before they can learn. They don't know how to work the new musculature."

"Some of them are just so awkward. It takes them months to learn the most simple things, like how to get enough water down with a bill. Cleaning themselves. I've seen some shocking cases. Just standing on one leg to scritch behind their head, that can take a lot of falling over before they get the method. And the lice drive them mad. It knocks the stuffing out of them.

We must never hand-feed them. We mustn't intervene too closely. That is one basic rule: we are there to give support but they have to learn. They never get it if you hand-feed them. We have to stand back. But it is hard to watch, isn't it?"

Bruce went on, "It is wonderful having you volunteers. It makes my job so much more manageable. Although they aren't all as sensible as you, Cat" Bruce said. "We have to be so strict. I'd lose my job if they caught me helping the poor old LTs. And overall, I like this work. It is always interesting, even when you feel sorry for them."

As a volunteer, Cat could break the rules and Bruce didn't need to notice. Bruce liked having Cat to give a helping hand and she felt better, she really did feel better, going round with him in the van.

The day it happened, they'd pulled in to a stand of manuka scrub where two kiwis who had been literalised were waiting for them. It was dusk, last call.

The two literalised kiwis were waiting at the edge of the ti-tree. They stood watching as Cat and Bruce approached, Bruce with the hemp sack of live bugs. He set the bag down on the wet grass.

Philip, the male, strode forward, gawky, but stronger at running than he had been last week. He was determined. Cat liked him the best of the two kiwis because he tried so hard. He was a young male, strutty, but methodical too. He could be used as a model for other avian LTs. Marion, who had previously been an accountant, was more tentative, not just passive, but almost sullen. Cat thought Marion was deeply depressed.

Marion stood back helplessly as Bruce opened the bag a little and a few insects sprang out. Philip darted forward and snatched something up. Cat couldn't quite see what it was he got. She got the impression of straggling legs and feelers. It happened in a flash. Philip really was good. She could see it wriggling in his throat as he held his head back and practised swallowing.

Cat held a squirming huhu bug out to Marion who eyed it with her head on one side. She looked, thought no, then awkwardly took it in her beak and shook it before gulping it down. Cat felt that Marion's hunger over-rode her will to just die rather than learn to forage for grubs in the wild. Eating to live was instinct.

The food had seemed to be grasshoppers but catching one that was getting away, Cat found it was a small sardine flapping off out of the sack and skywards. It writhed in protest in her hand. As the sack opened, pouring forth its flurry, Cat picked out a huge one. Its tail had been torn off, and the rich wet pink of its flesh looked, well, rather appetising even to a human. She held it out to Philip. "I'm not eating that," he said matter-of-factly. Cat looked again and could see his point: it was way too large for his gullet and it was also an unnatural food. Kiwis live in the bush and eat insects.

But she gathered, too, that he didn't like the fact that the sardine was not whole, but damaged, probably painfully. Healthy was better, live and kicking. You aimed for wellness in choosing the food.

Cat decided that she rather admired Philip. She was not sure how she had heard his thinking as communication in her own mind, but she was in accord with him. And Marion was so hopeless that you could not help feeling for her. There for the grace of God. Transformation had a long history of difficulty and more people these days were getting caught up in it. Speculation linked the increase to climate change. Not everyone can handle it. Cat gave Marion another small struggling morsel, helping her a little and signalling empathy.

The sardines were flying out thick and fast, skittering skyward.

Philip seemed to be changing again. His face rounded and toughened. That forceful beak had gone. His scales were quite beautiful, healthy, almost iridescent. He radiated. Cat found she was floating. She hadn't noticed. She had been so intent on watching Philip. He was changing before her eyes.

The water felt comfortable, and she had relaxed. As a salmon, Philip was enormous. She could see he was powerful. She was not afraid of him.

She floated on her back, and Philip hovered over her. His strong capable body hovered just a little above her, not quite touching. But she felt intensely aware of his firmness, the shimmering of his scales and his glowingness. She was watching him, fascinated, but he had gone out of focus as he grew larger and closer.

His colour was beautiful, although she had forgotten the word for it. All she could think of was "ripe,"' but that wasn't quite a colour.

And the colour that he was was so intense. She felt it warmly through her whole being. She was pulled by a strong tide. For the first time in her life Cat felt an urge, no, it was stronger than that, an uncontrollable compulsion, to let her eggs go sweetly and hopefully in a rush out into the water.

Here's one final text-box to take the book's exegesis back to your reality. What restores *you*, body, mind, heart and soul as you balance your work and your life?

My text-box-enclosed suggestions aim to remind you of the importance of self-restoration, wanting to tug your imagination to go further. How do you draw strength from and for your **body**?

- yoga, tai chi, Pilates, stretching, running, swimming, team sport, cycling, climbing hills,
- wearing comfortable shoes, warm clothes, cotton and silk clothes, socks that keep your feet dry, clothes that make you feel who you really are,
- taking care with what you eat, ensuring that you sleep well,
- massage,
- unguents, good hair products, natural oils,
- eating what you love, savouring chocolate, ripe fruit, special food that means home, greens you can feel flowing through your veins, that glass of wine, the right drugs, shared food, food that really is prepared with love,
- through snuggling, through dancing, through eye-to-eye contact, through touch and taste.

How do you maintain your **mind**, and feed it?

- reading for pleasure as well as for work,
- doing cryptic crosswords and Sudoku puzzles,
- travel,
- learning about music and art,
- figuring why to all the questions you ask yourself,
- writing to think,
- writing poetry and fiction,
- painting, singing, dancing,
- mindfulness,
- learning another language…

Your **heart** and your **soul**, how do you consciously grow these for your "work/life balance"

- Through the beauty of art, the beauty of the bush, the hills, the sea, the shoreline, through the beauty of the sky at dawn and in the evening,
- Through music, through poetry, through your place in your family, in your community, through singing, playing music,
- Through caring for those who can use your help, through forgiving, through giving, through noticing how rich, how beautiful, how right some aspects of your life are…

References

Abrams, M. H. (1993). (General Ed.) Shelley's defence of poetry. In *The Norton anthology of English literature* (Vol. II, 6th ed., pp. 753–765). New York, NY: Norton.

Downes, S. (2012). *Connectivism and connective knowledge: Essays on meaning and learning networks*. Stephen Downes Web. Available at http://www.downes.ca/files/Connective_Knowledge-19May2012.pdf

Harré, N., Grant, B. M., Locke, K., & Sturm, S. (2017). The university as an infinite game: Revitalising activism in the academy. *Australian Universities Review, 59*(2), 5–13.

Johnson, M. (1987). *The body in the mind: The bodily basis of meaning, imagination and reason*. Chicago, IL: University of Chicago Press.

Lakoff, G., & Johnson, M. (2003). *Metaphors we live by* (2nd ed.). Chicago, IL: University of Chicago Press.

Negus, K., & Pickering, M. (2004). *Creativity, communication and cultural value*. London, UK: Sage.

Thomas, L. M. & Reinertsen, A. B. (2019). A democratic ontology of knowledge: All of us slipping out the back door. In Thomas, L. M., & Reinertsen, A. B. (Eds.) *Academic writing and identity constructions: Performativity, space and territory in academic workplaces* (pp. 195–199). Cham, Switzerland: Palgrave Macmillan.

Pittman, K. (2005). I know what to look for. In K. A. Welsch (Ed.), *Those Winter Sundays: Female Academics and their Working Class Parents* (pp. 148–160). Maryland, Ma.: University of America Press.

Punter, D. (2007). *Metaphors*. London, UK: Routledge.

References

Abrams, M. H. (1993). (General Ed.) Shelley's defence of poetry. In *The Norton anthology of English literature* (Vol. II, 6th ed., pp. 753–765). New York, NY: Norton.

Acker, S., & Armenti, C. (2004). Sleepless in academia. *Gender and Education, 16*(1), 4–24.

Ahmed, S. (2006). *Queer phenomenology: Orientations, objects, others.* Durham, UK: Durham University Press.

Ahmed, S., & Stacey, J. (2001a). Introduction: Dermographics. In S. Ahmed & J. Stacey (Eds.), *Thinking through the skin* (pp. 1–17). New York, NY: Routledge.

Ahmed, S., & Stacey, J. (2001b). *Thinking through the skin.* London, UK: Routledge.

Aitchison, C., Catterall, J., Ross, P. I., & Burgin, S. (2012). "Tough love and tears": Learning doctoral writing in the sciences. *Higher Education Research & Development, 31*(4), 435–447.

Aitchison, C., & Guerin, C. (2014). Writing groups, pedagogy, theory, practice: An introduction. In C. Aitchison & C. Guerin (Eds.), *Writing groups for doctoral education and beyond: Innovations in theory and practice* (pp. 3–17). London, UK: Routledge.

Aitchison, C., & Lee, A. (2006). Research writing: Problems and pedagogies. *Teaching in Higher Education, 11*(3), 265–278.

AkldUni4Schools. (2010). University of Auckland lecturer on unicycle with student on his shoulders – juggling!!!. Retrieved from https://www.youtube.com/watch?v=PuhhpBJtMTw

S. Carter, *Academic Identity and the Place of Stories*,
https://doi.org/10.1007/978-3-030-43601-8

Albrecht, W. P. (Ed.). (1954). *Thomas of Erceldoune: The Loathly Lady in Thomas of Erceldoune with a text of the poem printed in 1652*. Albuquerque, NM: University of New Mexico.

Alexander, K. (2005). Liminal identities and institutional positioning: On becoming a "writing lady" in the academy. *Inkshed, 22*(3), 5–16.

Amundsen, C., & McAlpine, L. (2011). New academics as supervisors: A steep learning curve with challenges, tensions and pleasures. In L. McAlpine & C. Amundsen (Eds.), *Doctoral education: Research-based strategies for doctoral students, supervisors and administrators* (pp. 37–55). Dordrecht, The Netherlands: Springer.

Anae, M. S. (2010). Teu le va: Toward a 'native' anthropology. *Pacific Studies, 33*(2), 222–240.

Anzaldua, G. (1987). *Borderlands/La Frontera: The new Mestiza*. San Francisco, CA: Aunt Lute Books.

Archer, L. (2008). Younger academics' constructions of "authenticity", "success" and professional identity. *Studies in Higher Education, 33*(4), 385–403.

Atkinson, N. (2005). The ever present past. In K. A. Welsch (Ed.), *Those winter Sundays: Female academics and their working class parents* (pp. 84–92). Lanham, MD: University of America Press.

Augustine. (1838). The confessions of S. Augustine (E. B. Pusey, Trans.). In E. B. Pusey (Ed.), *The Confessions of S. Augustine* (Vol. 1). Oxford, UK: J. H. Parker.

Austin, A. E. (2002). Creating a bridge to the future: Preparing new faculty to face changing expectations in a shifting context. *The Review of Higher Education, 26*(2), 119–144.

Badenhorst, C., & Guerin, C. (2016). *Research literacies and writing pedagogies for masters and doctoral writers*. Leiden, The Netherlands: Studies in Writing Series, Brill.

Bakhtin, M. M. T. C. (1968). *Rabelais and his world* (H. Iswolsky, Trans.). Cambridge, MA: MIT Press.

Ball, S. J. (2003). The teacher's soul and the terrors of performativity. *Journal of Education Policy, 18*(2), 215–228.

Barcan, R. (2013). *Academic life and the new university: Hope and other choices*. Surrey, UK: Ashgate Publishing.

Barnett, R. (2000). University knowledge in an age of supercomplexity. *Higher Education, 40*, 409–422.

Barry, J., Berg, E., & Chandler, J. (2006). Academic shape-shifting: Gender, management and identities in Sweden and England. *Organization, 13*(2), 275–308.

Becher, T., & Trowler, P. (2001). *Academic tribes and territories: Intellectual enquiry and the culture of disciplines* (2nd ed.). Philadelphia, PA: Open University Press.

Bell, M., & Cooper, P. (2013). Peer observation of teaching in university departments: A framework for implementation. *International Journal for Academic Development, 18*(1), 60–73.

Benson, L. D. (Ed.). (1987). *The riverside Chaucer*. Oxford, UK: Oxford University Press.

Berg, M., & Seeber, B. M. (2017). *The slow professor: Challenging the culture of speed in the academy*. Toronto, ONT: University of Toronto Press.

Berne, E. (1967). *Games people play*. New York: Grove Press.

Bernstein, D. J. (2008). Peer review and the evaluation of the intellectual work of teaching. *Change, 40*(2), 48–51.

Bill, A. (2017). Counter-conduct in creative university research: Deliberations on freedom. *Higher Education Research & Development, 36*(2), 241–254.

Billot, J. (2010). The imagined and the real: The tensions for academic identity. *Higher Education and Research Development, 29*(6), 709–721.

Bloom, B. S. (1965). *Taxonomy of educational objectives: The classification of educational goals*. New York, NY: David McKay.

Boice, R. (1990). *Professors as writers: A self-help guide to productivity*. Stillwater, OK: New Forums.

Bosanquet, A., Mailey, A., Matthews, K. E., & Lodge, J. M. (2016). Redefining 'early career in academia: A collective narrative approach. *Higher Education and Research Development, 36*(5), 890–902.

Boyd, E. R. (2019). How creativity can help us create moral imagination. The Conversation. Available at https://eveningreport.nz/2019/01/30/how-creativity-can-help-us-cultivate-moral-imagination-101968/.

Brailsford, I. (2011). "The ha'porth of tar to save the ships": Student counselling and vulnerable university students. *History of Education, 40*(3), 357–370.

Brookfield, S. D. (2006). *The skillfull teacher: On technique, trust, and responsiveness in the classroom* (2nd ed.). San Francisco, CA: Jossey-Bass.

Brothe, C. (2005). You ain't ever gonna be better than me. In K. A. Welsch (Ed.), *Those winter Sundays: Female academics talk about their working class Parents* (pp. 13–20). Lanham, MD: University Press of America.

Brown, L., & Watson, P. (2010). Understanding the experience of female doctoral students. *Journal of Further and Higher Education, 34*(3), 385–404.

Bruffee, K. A. (1999). *Collaborative learning: Higher education, interdependence, and the authority of knowledge* (2nd ed.). Baltimore, MD: The Johns Hopkins Press.

Bynum, C. W. (1991). *Fragmentation and redemption: Essays on gender and the human body in medieval religion*. New York, NY: Zone Books.

Calvino, I. (1993). *If on a winter's night a traveler*. London, UK: Minerva.

Cantwell, R. (2011). Academic in-sourcing: International postdoctoral employment and new modes of academic production. *Journal of Higher Education Policy and Management, 33*(2), 102–114.

Cantwell, R., & Scevak, J. (2010). *An academic life: A handbook for new academics.* Camberwell, UK: ACER.
Carroll, L. (1871). *Through the looking-glass.* London, UK: Macmillan.
Carruthers, M. J. (1990). *The book of memory: A study of memory in medieval culture.* Cambridge, UK: Cambridge University Press.
Carruthers, M. J., & Ziolkowski, J. M. (Eds.). (2002). *The medieval craft of memory: An anthology of texts and pictures.* Philadelphia, PA: University of Pennsylvania Press.
Carter, S. (2008). Examining the doctoral thesis: A discussion. *Innovations in Education and Teaching International, 45*(4), 365–374.
Carter, S. (2011). Mapping monstrous desire: Flirting with Sir Gawain. In N. Hoofnagle & W. R. Keller (Eds.), *Other nations: The hybridization of medieval insular mythology and identity* (pp. 165–184). Heidelberg, Germany: Universitätsverlag Winter.
Carter, S. (2012). Original knowledge, gender and the word's mythology: Voicing the doctorate. *Arts and Humanities in Higher Education, 11*(4), 406–417.
Carter, S. (2014). The methodology of magpies. *International Journal of Research & Method in Education, 37*(2), 125–136.
Carter, S. & Pitcher, R. (2010). Extended metaphors for pedagogy: Using sameness and difference. *Teaching in Higher Education, 15*(5), 579–589.
Carter, S., Blumenstein, M., & Cook, C. (2013). Different for women?: The challenges of doctoral study. *Teaching in Higher Education, 18*(4), 339–351.
Carter, S., Kensington-Miller, B., & Courtney, M. (2017a). Doctoral supervision practice: What's the problem and how can we help academics? *Journal of Perspectives in Applied Academic Practice, 5*(1), 13–22. https://doi.org/10.14297/jpaap.v5i1.235
Carter, S., & Laurs, D. (Eds.). (2014). *Developing Generic Support for Doctoral Students: Practice and Pedagogy.* London/New York: Routledge.
Carter, S., Laurs, D., Chant, L., Wolfgramm-Foliaki, E., Martin, J., Teaiwa, T. et al. (2016). *Research report supporting doctoral writing: He ara tika mā ngā kaiārahi.* Retrieved from https://akoaotearoa.ac.nz/doctoral-writing-feedback
Carter, S., Laurs, D., Chant, L., & Wolgramm-Foliaki, E. (2017b). Indigenous knowledge and supervision: Changing the lens. *Innovations in Education and Teaching International, 55*(3), 384–393. https://doi.org/10.1080/14703297.2017.1403941
Carter, S., & Poole, R. (2012). Threshold to discipline discourse: An English literature first year course. *Australian Journal of Language and Literacy, 35*(1), 69–81.
Carter, S., & Rod, P. (2010). Extended metaphors for pedagogy: Using sameness and difference. *Teaching in Higher Education, 15*(5), 579–589.
Chanock, K. (1995). Counselling and academic skills teaching: What person-centred counselling can tell us about person-centred skills teaching. In M. Garner, K. Chanock, & R. Clerehan (Eds.), *Academic skills advising: Towards a discipline* (pp. 29–37). Melbourne, VIC: Victorian Language and Learning Network.

Chanock, K., East, J., & Maxwell, J. (2004). Academic and/or general? How the classification of LAS advisors affects us and our institutions. *Language and Academic Skills in Higher Education, 6*, 37–45.

Chant, L. (2013). *Hauora Kotahitanga. Maori health experiences as models for co-operative co-existence between indigenous and non-indigenous peoples.* Doctoral dissertation, Auckland: University of Auckland. Available at https://researchspace.auckland.ac.nz/

Child, F. J. (Ed.). (1882). *The English and Scottish popular ballads.* New York, NY: Pageant.

Churchman, D. (2006). Institutional commitments, individual compromises: Identity-related responses to compromise in an Australian university. *Journal of Higher Education Policy and Management, 28*(1), 3–5.

Churchman, D., & King, S. (2009). Academic practice in transition: Hidden stories of academic identities. *Teaching in Higher Education, 14*(5), 507–516.

Cleveland-Innes, M., & Campbell, P. (2012). Emotional presence, learning, and the online learning environment. *The International Review of Research in Open and Distance Learning, 13*(4), 269–292.

Collini, S. (2013). Sold out. *London Review of Books, 35*, 3–12. Retrieved from https://www.lrb.co.uk/v35/n20/stefan-collini/sold-out

Constantine, P. (2008). (Trans. & Ed.) *The Prince: Niccolò Machiavelli 1469–1527.* New York: The Modern Library.

Cosh, J. (1998). Peer observation: A reflective model. *ELT Journal, 53*(1), 22–27.

Davies, W. (Ed. (1979). *Gerard Manley Hopkins: The major poems.* London: J. M. Dent & Sons.

Debowski, S. (2012). *The new academic: A strategic handbook.* New York, NY: Open University Press.

Dinshaw, C. (1999). *Getting medieval: Sexualities and communities, pre- and post-modern.* Durham, NC: Duke University Press.

Donaldson, E. T. (1993). The Battle of Maldon. In M. H. Abrams (Ed.), *The Norton anthology: English literature* (Vol. 1, pp. 70–75). New York, NY: W. W. Norton and Co..

Downes, S. (2012). *Connectivism and connective knowledge: Essays on meaning and learning networks.* Stephen Downes Web. Available at http://www.downes.ca/files/Connective_Knowledge-19May2012.pdf

Elbow, P. P. (1998). *Writing with power: Techniques for mastering the writing process.* Oxford, UK: Oxford University Press.

Eliot, T. S. (1968). *Four quartets.* London, UK: Folio Society.

Fellows, J. (Ed.). (1993). *Of love and chivalry: An anthology of middle English romances.* London, UK: Dent.

Finke, L. A. (1992). *Feminist theory, women's writing.* Ithaca, NY: Cornell University Press.

Finke, R. A., & Bettle, J. (1996). *Chaotic cognition: Principles and applications.* Mahwah, NJ: Lawrence Erlbaum Associates.

Flavell, J. H. (1979). Metacognition and cognitive monitoring: A new area of cognitive-developmental Inquiry. *American Psychologist, 34*(10), 906–911.

Fowler, H. W. (1952). *A dictionary of modern English usage*. Oxford, UK: Clarendon.

Freire, P. (1998). *Pedagogy of freedom: Ethics, democracy, and civic courage*. Oxford, UK: Rowman & Littlefield.

Frye, N. (1982). *The great code: the Bible and literature* (1st ed.). New York, NY: Harcourt Brace Jovanovich.

Fyffe, J. M. (2018). Getting comfortable with being uncomfortable: A narrative account of becoming an academic developer. *International Journal of Academic Development, 23*(4), 355–366.

Garrett, G., & Davies, G. (2010). *Herding cats: Being advice to aspiring academic and research leaders*. Axminster, UK: Triarchy Press.

Garrison, D. R., Anderson, T., & Archer, W. (2000). Critical inquiry in a text-based environment: Computer conferencing in higher education. *The Internet and Higher Education, 2*(2–3), 87–105.

Geertsema, J., & Laksov, K. B. (2019). Turning challenges into opportunities: (Re-)vitalizing the role of academic development. *International Journal for Academic Development, 24*(1), 1–6.

Gill, R. (2009). Breaking the silence: The hidden injuries of neo-liberal academia. In R. Flood & R. Gill (Eds.), *Secrecy and silence in the research process: Feminist reflections* (pp. 228–244). London, UK: Routledge.

Golding, C. (2013). Must we gather data? A place for the philosophical study of higher education. *Higher Education Research Development, 32*(1), 152–155.

Gopen, G. D. (2017). How to improve your advisees' writing permanently—in 30 minutes. In S. Carter & D. Laurs (Eds.), *Developing research writing: A handbook for supervisors and advisors* (pp. 77–86). London, UK: Routledge.

Gopen, G. G. (2018). How to improve your advisees' writing permanently—in 30 minutes. In Carter, S. and Laurs, D. (Eds.) *Developing research writing: A handbook for supervisors and advisors*. Oxon: Routledge, 77–86.

Gopen, G. D., & Swan, J. (1990). The science of scientific writing. *American Scientist, 78*(6), 550–558.

Grant, B., & Barrow, M. (2013). Fashioning docile teacher bodies? The strange space of the "staff teaching seminar". *International Journal for Academic Development, 18*(4), 306–317.

Graves, R. (Ed.). (1957). *English and Scottish ballads*. London, UK: Heinemann.

Guerin, C., & Green, I. (2016). Cultural diversity and the imagined community of the global academy. *Asia Pacific Journal of Education, 36*(1). https://doi.org/10.1080/02188791.2014.922048

Hall, D. E. (2007). *The academic community: A manual for change*. Columbus, OH: Ohio State Press.

Hamilton, A. C. (Ed.). (1997). *The Spenser encyclopedia*. Toronto, ONT: University of Toronto Press.

Harré, N., Grant, B. M., Locke, K., & Sturm, S. (2017). The university as an infinite game: Revitalising activism in the academy. *Australian Universities Review, 59*(2), 5–13.

Harris, P., Thiele, B., & Currie, J. (1998). Success, gender and academic voices: Consuming passion or selling the soul? *Gender and Education, 10*(2), 133–148.

Harris, S. (2006). Rethinking academic identities in neo-liberal times. *Teaching in Higher Education, 10*(4), 421–433.

Hau'ofa, E. (2008). *We are the ocean: Selected works.* Honolulu, HA: University of Haiwai'i Press.

Heaney, S. (2000). *Beowulf.* New York, NY: Farrar, Straus & Giroux.

Heifetz, R. A., & Linsky, M. (2002). *Leadership on the line: Staying alive through the dangers of leading.* Boston, MA: Harvard Business School Press.

Henderson, C. (2013). *The book of barely imagined beings: A 21st century bestiary.* Chicago, IL: University of Chicago.

Honan, E. (2017). Producing moments of pleasure within the confines of the Neoliberal University. In S. Riddle, M. K. Harmes, & P. A. Danaher (Eds.), *Producing pleasure in the Contemporary University* (pp. 13–24). Rotterdam/Boston/Taipei: Sense.

hooks, b. (1991). Theory as liberatory practice. *Yale Journal of Feminism and Law, 4*(1), 1–13.

Jack, G. (Ed.). (1994). *Beowulf: A student edition.* Oxford, UK: Clarendon.

Johnson, M. (1987). *The body in the mind: The bodily basis of meaning, imagination and reason.* Chicago, IL: University of Chicago Press.

Jones, S. H., Adams, T. E., & Ellis, C. (2016). *Handbook of autoethnography.* London, UK: Routledge.

Kaili, T. O. (2005). Tauhi va: Nurturing Tongan sociospatial ties in maui and beyond. *The Contemporary Pacific, 17*(1), 83–114.

Kaili, T. O. (2008). Tauhi va: Creating beauty through the art of sociospatial relations. PhD Dissertation. Seattle: University of Washington.

Kamler, B., & Thomson, P. (2006). *Helping doctoral students write: Pedagogies for supervision.* London, UK: Routledge.

Kearns, H., & Gardiner, M. (2007). Is it time well spent? The relationship between time management behaviours, perceived effectiveness and work-related morale and distress in a university context. *Higher Education Research and Development, 26*(2), 235–247.

Kelly, F. (2015). A day in the life (and death) of a public university. *Higher Education Research Development, 34*(6), 1153–1163.

Kelly, F. (2017). *The idea of the PhD: The doctorate in the twenty-first century.* London, UK: Routledge.

Kendig, D. (2005). The seams that stood all the changes: Keeping it together in academia. In K. A. Welsch (Ed.), *Those winter Sundays: Female academics and their working class parents* (pp. 1–12). Lanham, MD: University Press of America.

Kensington-Miller, B., & Carter, S. (2019). 'Permission to write': Building a community of inter-disciplinary writers. *Journal of Perspectives in Applied Academic Practice, 7*(1), 1–10.

Kidman, F., Chu, C., Fernandez, S., & Abella, I. (2015). *Māori scholars and the university*. Wellington, NZ: Victoria University of Wellington.

King, S. (2000). *On writing: A memoir of the craft*. New York, NY: Scribener.

King, V. (2003). Self-portrait with mortar board: A study of academic identity using the map, the novel and the grid. *Higher Education Research & Development, 32*(1), 96–108.

Kirby, V. (1994). Response to Jane Gallop's "The Teacher's Breasts": Bad form. In J. J. Matthews (Ed.), *Jane Gallop seminar papers: Proceedings of the Jane Gallop Seminar and public lecture "The Teacher's Breasts"* (pp. 17–22). Canberra, ACT: Humanities Research Centre.

Kogan, M. (2000). Higher education communities and academic identity. *Higher Education Quarterly, 54*(3), 207–216.

Lakoff, G., & Johnson, M. (2003). *Metaphors we live by* (2nd ed.). Chicago, IL: University of Chicago Press.

Lamott, A. (1995). *Bird by bird: Some instructions for writing and life*. New York, NY: Anchor.

Laurs, D., & Carter, S. (2013, November). *Learning advisors and doctoral border-crossing: Negotiating those frontiers*. Paper presented at the Annual International Conference of the Association of Tertiary Learning Advisors of Aotearoa/New Zealand, Christchurch.

Lister, R. (2016). Citizenship, welfare rights and local government. In J. Demaine & H. Entwistle (Eds.), *Beyond communitarianism: Citizenship, politics and education* (pp. 163–178). Basingstoke, UK: Palgrave Macmillan.

Macaulay, G. C. (Ed.). (1899). *Confessio amantis. The complete works of John Gower*. Oxford, UK: Clarendon.

MacFarlane, B. (2007). *The academic citizen: The virtue of service in university life*. London, UK: Routledge.

Mahina, O. (2010). Ta, va, and moana: Temporality, spatiality and indigeneity. *Pacific Studies, 33*(2, 3), 168–202.

Manathunga, C. (2007). "Unhomely" academic developer identities: More post-colonial explorations. *International Journal for Academic Development, 12*(1), 25–34.

Marsh, D. R., Schroeder, D. G., Dearden, K. A., & Sternin, M. (2004). The power of positive deviance. *British Medical Journal, 329*, 1177–1179.

Martin, P. (1992). Chaucer and feminism: A magpie view. In J. Dor (Ed.), *"A wyf ther was": Essays in honour of Paule Mertens-Frock* (pp. 235–246). Liege, Belgium: University of Liege Press.

Marton, F., & Saljo, R. (1976). On qualitative differences in learning: Outcome and process. *British Journal of Educational Psychology, 46*, 4–11.

McLean, K. C., & Pasupathi, M. (2012). Process of identity: Where I am and how I got there. *An International Journal of Theory and Research, 12*(1), 8–28.

McNair, S. (1997). Is there a crisis? Does it matter? In R. Barnett & A. Griffin (Eds.), *The end of knowledge in higher education* (pp. 27–38). London, UK: Cassell.

Mewburn, I. (2011). Is the university a bad boyfriend? Retrieved from https://thesiswhisperer.com/2011/08/09/is-the-university-a-bad-boyfriend/

Meyer, J. H. F., & Land, R. (2005). Threshold concepts and troublesome knowledge (2): Epistemological considerations and a conceptual framework for teaching and learning. *Higher Education, 39*, 373–388.

Middleton, S. (2009). Becoming PBRF-able: Research assessment and education in New Zealand. In T. Besley (Ed.), *Assessing the quality of research in higher education: International perspective* (pp. 193–208). Rotterdam, The Netherlands: Sense Publishers.

Mitchell, C. (2006, November). *A + B = 1:1, formula required? Reflections on learning development and one-to-one teaching from a new learning development tutor.* Paper presented at the Anchoring our practice: Perspectives, partnerships, projections, Tauranga.

Morley, L. (2003). *Quality and power in higher education.* Philadelphia, PA: Society for Research into Higher Education & Open University Press.

Negus, K., & Pickering, M. (2004). *Creativity, communication and cultural value.* London, UK: Sage.

Orwell, G. (1946). *Politics and the English language.* London, UK: Horizon.

Overfield, D. (1995). *The economics of social subordination: Gender relations and market failure in the highlands of Papua New Guinea.* Unpublished doctoral thesis, University of London, England.

Paltridge, B., & Harbon, L. (2006, November). *Intercultural competencies and the international experience.* Paper presented at the Communication Skills in University Education Auckland, New Zealand.

Parry, S. (2007). *Disciplines and doctorates* (Vol. 16). Dordrecht, The Netherlands: Springer.

Passmore, S. E. (2007). Through the counsel of a lady: The Irish and English Loathly Lady tales and the "Mirrors for princes" genre. In S. E. Passmore & S. Carter (Eds.), *The "English Loathly Lady" tales: Boundaries, traditions, motifs* (pp. 3–41). Kalamazoo, MI: Medieval Institute Press.

Pelias, R. J. (2004). *A methodology of the heart: Evoking academic and daily life.* New York, NY: AltaMira Press.

Petersen, E. B. (2012, June). *Monsters astray in the flesh: A layered exploration of the im/possibilities of resistance-work in the neoliberalised university.* Paper presented at the Academic Identities Conference, University of Auckland.

Phillips, N., & Hardy, C. (2002). *Discourse analysis: Investigating processes of social construction.* London, UK: Sage.

Phipps, A. (2013). Intercultural ethics: Questions of methods in language and intercultural communication. *Language and Intercultural Communication, 13*(1), 10–26.

Pinker, S. (2015). *The sense of style: The thinking person's guide to writing in the 21st century*. New York, NY: Penguin.

Pittman, K. (2005). I know what to look for. In K. A. Welsch (Ed.), *Those Winter Sundays: Female Academics and their Working Class Parents* (pp. 148–160). Maryland, Ma.: University of America Press.

Pogue Harrison, R. (1992). *Forests: The shadow of civilization*. Chicago, IL: Chicago University Press.

Punter, D. (2007). *Metaphors*. London, UK: Routledge.

Raabe B, Frese, M & Beehr, T. A. (2007). Action regulation theory and career self-management. *Journal of Vocational Behavior, 70*(2): 297–311.

Reinertsen, A. B. & Thomas, L. M. (2019). A democratic ontology of knowledge: All of us slipping out the back door. In Thomas, L. M., & Reinertsen, A. B. (Eds.) *Academic writing and identity constructions: Performativity, space and territory in academic workplaces* (pp. 195–199). Cham, Switzerland: Palgrave Macmillan.

Reiss, S. (2012). Intrinsic and extrinsic motivation. *Teaching of Philosophy, 39*(2), 152–156.

Ruccio, D. F. (2017). Academic precariat. Retrieved from https://rwer.wordpress.com/2017/04/16/academic-precariat/

Rudd, E., Morrison, E., Sadrozinski, R., Nerad, M., & Cerny, J. (2008). Equality and illusion: Gender and tenure in art history careers. *Journal of Marriage and Family, 70*(1), 228–238.

Ruggiers, P. G. (Ed.). (1979). *Chaucer, Geoffrey. The Canterbury tales: A facsimile and transcription of the Hengwrt manuscript with variants from the Ellesmere manuscript*. Norman, OK: University of Oklahoma.

Samuels, L. (2002). Relinquish intellectual property. *New Literary History, 33*(2), 357–374.

Schiltz, D. (1976). The Gambler. [Recorded by Music City Roots].

Shea, P., & Bidjerano, T. (2009). Community of inquiry as a theoretical framework to foster "epistemic engagement" and "cognitive presence" in online education. *Computers & Education, 52*(3), 543–553.

Shore, C., & Wright, S. (2017). Privatizing the public university: Key trends, countertrends and alternatives. In S. Wright & C. Shore (Eds.), *Death of the public university? Uncertain futures for higher education in the knowledge economy* (pp. 1–27). New York/Oxford: Berghahn Books.

Siddiqui, Z. S., Jonas-Dwyer, D., & Carr, S. E. (2007). Twelve tips for peer observation of teaching. *Medical Teacher, 29*, 297–800.

Silvia, P. (2010). *How to write a lot: A practical guide to productive academic writing* (6th ed.). Washington, DC: APA Life Tools.

Smith, G. H. (1990). *Tomorrow's schools and the development of Māori education*. Paper presented at the Second Educational Policy Conference, New Zealand Council for Educational Research. Reprinted in *Research Unit for Māori Education*, monograph no. 5, December 1991, The University of Auckland.

Smith, L. T. (1999). *Decolonizing methodologies: Research and indigenous peoples.* New York, NY: Zed Books.

Somers, M. R. (1993). Citizenship and the place of the public sphere: Law, community, and political culture in the transition to democracy. *American Sociological Review, 58*(5), 587–620.

Sparkes, A. C. (2007). Embodiment, academics and the audit culture: A story seeking consideration. *Qualitative Research, 7*(4), 521–550.

Stokes, W. (1903). The death of Crimthann son of Fidach, and the adventures of the sons of Eochaid Muigmedon. *Revue Celtique, 24*, 172–207.

Stokes, W., & Windisch, E. (Eds.). (1887). *Coir Anmann. Fitness of names.* Leipzig, Germany: Hirzel.

Strunk, W., Jr., & White, E. B. (2000). *The elements of style* (4th ed.). Boston, MA: Allyn and Bacon.

Sturm, S., & Carter, S. (2015). From Eden to Agora: The e-learning trading zone. *Critical Studies in Teaching and Learning (CriSTaL), 3*(2), 40–59. https://doi.org/10.14426/cristal.v3i2.48

Suits, B. (1978). *The grasshopper: Games, life and utopia.* Toronto, ONT: University of Toronto Press.

Sutton, P. (2014). A paradoxical academic identity: Fate, utopia and hope. *Teaching in Higher Education, 20*(1), 37–47. https://doi.org/10.1080/13562517.2014.957265

Swartz, P. C. (2005). "A circle" or, strangely, a life in school. In K. A. Welsch (Ed.), *Those winter Sundays: Female academics and their working class parents* (pp. 69–83). Lanham, MD: University of America Press.

Sword, H. (2007). *The writer's diet.* Auckland, NZ: Pearson Education NZ.

Sword, H. (2009). Writing higher education differently: A manifesto on style. *Studies in Higher Education, 34*(3), 319–336.

Sword, H. (2012, July 23). Zombie nouns. *The New York Times.* Retrieved from https://opinionator.blogs.nytimes.com/2012/07/23/zombie-nouns/

Sword, H. (2017). *Air and light and time and space.* Cambridge, MA: Harvard University Press.

Tate, P. H. (1999). *Workshop on Whanaungatanga.* September 8–9, Auckland: Te Hiku o te Ika Trust.

Taylor, C., Gannon, S., Adams, G., Donaghue, H., Hannam-Swain, S., Harris-Evans, J., et al. (2020). Grim tales: Meetings, matterings and moments of silencing and frustration in everyday academic life. *International Journal of Educational Research, 99*, 101513. https://doi.org/10.1016/j.ijer.2019.101513

Thaman, K. H. (2008). Education in Pacific Island Countries. In G. McCulloch & D. Crook (Eds.), *The Routledge International encyclopedia of education* (pp. 413–416). London/New York: Routledge.

Theodore, R., Tustin, K., Kiro, C., Gollop, M., Taumoepeau, M., Taylor, N., et al. (2016). Māori university graduates: Indigenous participation in higher education. *Higher Education Research and Development, 38*(3), 604–618.

Thesen, L. (2014). "If they're not laughing, watch out!": Emotion and risk in postgraduate writing groups. In C. Aitcheson & C. Guerin (Eds.), *Writing groups for the doctorate and beyond: Innovations in practice and theory* (pp. 172–176). London, UK: Routledge.

Thomas, L. M., & Reinertsen, A. B. (Eds.). (2019). *Academic writing and identity constructions: Performativity, space and territory in academic workplaces.* Cham, Switzerland: Palgrave Macmillan.

Tolkien, J. R. R. (2001). *The Lord of the Rings.* Boston, MA: Houghton Mifflin.

Van Rij-Heyligers, J. A. (2005). *Globalisation and pluri-scalar orchestrations in higher education: Locating the University of Auckland's Student Learning Centre historically and globally.* University of Auckland, NZ: EdD.

Watkins, D., & Biggs, J. B. (1996). *The Chinese learner: Cultural, psychological and contextual influences.* Hong Kong/Melbourne, VIC: University of Hong Kong Comparative Education Research Centre; Australian Council for Educational Research.

Webber, M. (2009). The multiple selves and realities of a Māori researcher. *Māori and Indigenous Review, 1*, 1–8.

Welsch, K. A. (Ed.). (2005). *Those winter Sundays: Female academics and their working class parents.* Lanham, MD: University Press of America.

Wheaton, A. (2020). Shift happens: Moving from the ivory tower to the mushroom factory. *Higher Education Research & Development, 39*(1), 67–80.

Winter, R. (2009). Academic manager or managed academic?: Academic identity schisms in Higher Education. *Journal of Higher Education Policy and Management, 31*(2), 121–131.

Wright, S., & Shore, C. (2017). *Death of the public university? Uncertain futures for higher education in the knowledge economy.* New York/Oxford: Berghahn Books.

Zandy, J. (2005). Foreword. In K. A. Welsch (Ed.), *Those winter Sundays: Female academics and their working class parents.* Lanham, MD: University Press of America.

Zhang, X. (2017). *Flying kites: How Chinese international students in New Zealand reflect on Chinese citizenship.* Doctoral thesis, University of Auckland, Auckland, New Zealand.

Index

S. Carter, *Academic Identity and the Place of Stories*,
https://doi.org/10.1007/978-3-030-43601-8

Printed by Printforce, the Netherlands